WALK TEN STEPS WITH THE LORD

C. THOMAS EBEL

PRESS

www.xulonpress.com

Dedication

This book is dedicated to the loving memory of my mother and father, Sis and Ebo, my aunt and uncle, Vera and Bob, and their daughter and my cousin, Ann, whose unconditional love for me gave a glimpse of the kind of love God has for all of us and that He wants us to share with one another.

Acknowledgements

I first want to thank my wife, Liz, whose love, support, companionship and guidance made this book possible. She loves the Lord more than anyone I know, and she loves me, with my many flaws, far beyond anything I deserve. She was the initial editor of each chapter of this book, providing invaluable direction and encouragement.

I also want to thank my small group, Blair, Earl, Steve, Stuart and Joel, with whom I have met just about every week for well into our second decade and who have been instrumental in strengthening my faith. Their insight and wisdom are reflected in this book. I am so grateful to them for continually encouraging me to push forward with this project.

I also want to thank Buddy Childress, the Director of Needle's Eye Ministries in Richmond, Virginia, who led me to know the Lord, and who read an early version of the book. He provided valuable observations and encouragement.

I want to express my appreciation to my law partner, turned evangelist, Doug Rucker, who took the time from his busy schedule to read the book and provide both substantive and, as always, grammatical comment.

I want to thank Fritz Kling, a friend and published Christian author, for his encouragement and advice about publishing.

I also am so very grateful to Steve Hartman, the head pastor at our church, Third Presbyterian Church in Richmond. Steve read the book and provided important suggestions. More significantly, he also does an outstanding job leading our church, where my faith in the Lord has been affirmed and strengthened.

I want to express my deep appreciation to Jon Wakefield, my final editor, whose advice and suggested revisions made this book much better. He was recommended to me by Steve Hartman, and I have no question the Lord was at work in putting us together.

Most of all, I want to thank God for providing the inspiration, vision, energy and means to finish writing this book. Please know it is His work, not mine.

Table of Contents

Introduction

Jesus Christ, a carpenter turned homeless rabbi, with no financial or worldly resources, began His three-year ministry not by choosing the religious elite or highly educated, but rather by calling as His disciples twelve ordinary working men, with no formal religious training. Look what they accomplished! From that remarkably humble beginning, the Christian faith spread over the entire world, changing the course of history. Today, Christianity numbers over two billion followers, more than any other religion.

For many years, I have struggled with how we can best perpetuate Jesus' original model today. How does a Christian believer in the modern world effectively explain God, Jesus Christ, the Bible and Christianity to someone seeking to know more about them? I have searched for a way to help others to know the same peace, joy, comfort, wisdom and transforming power I found in Jesus Christ. This book is a result of that struggle, explaining how I believe people can best be started on a journey of faith, which will feed their spiritual hunger, transform their lives and empower them to transform the lives of others, as Jesus and His disciples did over two thousand years ago.

I am not a pastor, missionary or trained theologian. In fact, I have no formal religious education at all. I am a lawyer by profession, which may place me among the least likely of candidates to write a book about God or any religious subject. This book, though, is about faith, not religion.

My sole qualification is having lived my life in response to God's Word, guided by His hand. And looking back, I now see that God had His hand on my life from the very beginning.

For many years, despite attending church, engaging in community affairs, and generally leading what most would call a "good life," I was largely unaware God was at work in my life, and I was not walking closely with Him. When I was thirty years old, though, some good friends shared their relationship with the Lord Jesus Christ with me, and I turned control of my life over to Him.

That commitment marked the beginning of my journey with the Lord, the point at which I began to see life very differently. As the Apostle Paul states in 2 Corinthians 5:17, "So if anyone is in Christ, there is a new creation, everything old has passed away; see, everything has become new." I became more aware of the work of God in my life. I began to see how I needed to stop walking alone and start walking with and obeying Him. And now I rejoice in how He has *always* been there for me, providing guidance, support, strength and blessings in the midst of tragedies and challenges.

I was an only child of two devoted parents who had been told they could never have children. I was born in 1954, at the height of the post World War II baby boom, and grew up in a loving home during the 1950s and 1960s in suburban Richmond, Virginia. I had a relatively normal childhood until I was seventeen and a senior in high school, when my father died of a massive heart attack. Two years later my mother died of brain cancer. In my sophomore year of college, I stood alone in the world with virtually no immediate family.

In the midst of great pain, however, I was not alone: God was present and at work. First, the unconditional love and strong values my parents had instilled in me remained a powerful and sustaining influence after their deaths. In addition, I was taken in by my father's sister, a strong Christian woman, and her family. They loved me unconditionally and still treat me today as a cherished member of their family. God also provided many other friends and family members to fill the void left by the absence of any immediate family. Today, I am blessed with a vast network of family, friends and colleagues beyond what I could have ever considered possible.

Then at age twenty-one, I met and fell in love with my wife Liz. As a strong Christian woman, she has helped me in many ways stay on the right path with the Lord. She has also been a loving and supportive partner and a valuable editor for this book.

We have been happily married for over three decades and have two fine children, a daughter and a son.

I want to make it clear, however, that my struggles, challenges and tragedies did not cease when I came to know Jesus Christ. In fact, they often intensified. Over the past several years, my family has faced its own struggles. We have seen the death of dear family members and friends at a young age, and Liz and I have mourned the separation and divorce of many of our closest friends.

I have experienced career challenges as well. After many early struggles, though, God has blessed me with a successful law practice at an excellent firm, giving me the privilege to work closely with others of strong faith.

As I look upon the tragic and joyous events in my life, I know they were not just a series of coincidences. My life is the work of the masterful hand of God, leading me as His servant on a great journey. Through the many struggles, he was and is teaching me eternal lessons and bringing me closer to Him.

I have come to believe there is no such thing as a "normal" life. Regardless of how healthy, wealthy, or how good you are, sooner or later you will face stressful and sometimes life-altering circumstances. Many today endure famine, violence, illness, pain, addiction, abuse and other turmoil far greater than I could ever imagine. Your life experiences may be more or less severe than mine or others. But whatever your circumstances, God is present to meet your needs.

Something has caused you to pick up this book and read it. My hope is it will help you see how God, through Jesus Christ and the Holy Spirit, is at work in your life calling you to respond to His guiding hand. You are on a journey walking with the Lord, whether you know it or not. Nothing is to be gained, but everything is to be lost, by ignoring Him. I hope and pray this book will cause you to honestly and diligently consider the vital, liberating and transforming impact faith in God through Jesus Christ will have on your life.

This book is designed to take you along a path you may have never traveled before. By definition, a path is a well-worn way along the ground, where others have previously walked. A journey of the Spirit with the Lord is no different: it may be unfamiliar to you, but many others have already walked it. Take great comfort that you are on a spiritual journey with Jesus Christ where you will reach a safe, certain and rewarding destination. Some steps along the path may be more difficult than others, and you may wander astray or need to stop and rest, but the path is well-marked, and others who have already traveled it will meet and guide you along the way.

Most importantly, the Lord will be with you throughout the journey, and if you need direction, all you have to do is ask. Jesus told us in Mathew 7:7 and 8, "Ask and it will be given to you; search and you will find; knock and the door will be opened for you. For everyone who asks receives, and everyone who searches finds, and for everyone who knocks the door will be opened." And Psalm 18:36 states, "You gave me a wide place for my steps under me, and my feet did not slip."

Following the Christian path, truly devoted to Jesus Christ, will take you in a direction far removed from that taken by most others in our society today. Like a steep mountain hike, you will encounter difficult and uncomfortable times, and you may wonder whether you will ever reach the summit. But the strength you gain from this arduous spiritual walk will allow you to travel to places you never thought possible. The depths of understanding, the peace and the joy you will come to know, are incomparable. Jesus warned us in Mathew 7:13 and 14: "Enter through the narrow gate; for the gate is wide and road is easy that leads to destruction, and there are many who take it. For the gate is narrow and the road is hard which leads to life, and there are few who find it."

Although the path you will be walking is well-traveled, the steps set forth in this book are based on my experience, and yours may be very different. The steps I have outlined are not the only ones, and your journey may include others, and they may be taken in a different order. As you will see, however, the steps we all must take are to believe in God, believe Jesus Christ is His Son, believe in the full truth revealed by the Bible and trust the Holy Spirit to guide you along your way. If you cannot at least follow these basic steps, you and I will not be taking the same journey, and much of what is in this book may not be helpful to you.

If you *are* prepared to attempt these basic steps, I encourage you to move through the book at your own pace. I recommend, though, that you walk, not run. The use of the word "walk" in the title of this book is intentional. Our relationship with God is repeatedly described in the Bible in terms of a walk with Him:

Happy are the people who know the festal shout, who walk, O Lord, in the light of your countenance. (Psalm 89:15)

Even though I walk through the darkest valley, I fear no evil; for you are with me; your rod and your staff—they comfort me. (Psalm 23:4)

He has told you, O mortal what is good; and what does the Lord require of you, but to do justice, and to love kindness and to walk humbly with your God? (Micah 6:8)

Walk while you have the light, so that the darkness may not overtake you. If you walk in the darkness, you do not know where you are going. (John 12:35)

Walking requires patience and diligence. A relationship with God will develop in His time at His pace. Stop, reflect, and reread whatever passages in this book you need to. I also encourage you to study the Scripture passages and other sources referenced. And at the end of each chapter, I have included

"Guiding Questions" designed to help you reflect upon how the issues addressed and truths revealed in what you read may apply to you and move you toward a deeper knowledge of and relationship with the Lord. My aim is to inspire you to search for God's truth beyond these pages. This book is merely the beginning of your inquiry into the ways of the Lord, not the end.

All I humbly ask is that you sincerely search for the truth, just as I did at the start of my own journey. Do not be afraid. You have nothing to lose or to fear. Jesus said to those who believed in Him, "you will know the truth, and the truth will set you free" (John 8:32). Yes, you will find freedom in God's truth—freedom from such things as anxiety, stress, insecurity, pain, oppression and obsession. Discover the great mystery of the freedom that comes from obedience to God. No matter what else you may have heard or experienced to this point, never lose sight of the reality that God loves you and wants only good for you.

Since you now have come to a spiritual trailhead, why not at least walk a few steps along the path and see where it leads you? God will be with you, and I hope you will find it a compelling, liberating and transforming journey. May the peace of the Lord be with you along the way.

Chapter One

I Am the Lord

I am the Lord your God, who brought you out of the land of Egypt, out of the house of slavery; you shall have no other gods before me. – Exodus 20:2

There is no better place in the Bible to begin our journey with the Lord than with the First of the Ten Commandments in which, through Moses, the Lord declared to his people that He was God, who delivered them from slavery, and commanded them to have no gods before Him. The first step in moving toward a relationship with the Lord is to examine our belief in the fundamental premise that God exists. Most people affirm that there is a Supreme Being, especially Christians who attend church every Sunday, and even those who attend only occasionally. Before reading any further, you should ask yourself this eternal question: Does God exist? If your answer is "yes," or even "I think so," you should read on. But understand you are making a profound decision: you affirm that a power greater than you made the universe, the earth and us, and is at work in the midst of our world, and in our very lives, at this very moment. If you are convinced there is no God, that is a courageous decision, and there may be little this book can do for you. But you may want to keep reading to test your conviction. You also may want to play along for while, just to see what difference it might make in your life if you pretended to believe for only a few hours or a couple of days. You might see things you never have before. You should test yourself to see whether you really want to live in a world where there is no God who would give you strength and joy, deliver you from very difficult circumstances (a slavery of your own?), if you really needed Him, and who would always love you, even when no one else does.

If you are ready to continue, you must determine what it means to decide that God exists. In the First Commandment, not only does God remind the Israelites that He is God, but also that it was He who delivered them out of Egypt and slavery. He then issues the commandment that they shall have no other gods before Him. Therefore, if you accept that God is God, you must recognize first that He is in control, not you. He is the one who delivers you from your own slavery, and you need only to look to Him to do so. But taking this step means you must have enough faith to let go and give up control of your life and let God into it.

What other gods do you have that are pushing the only true God out of your life? At first, it may seem easy to claim that you have no other gods. You probably do not believe in a Sun god or a Wind god or Zeus or some other kind of pagan god, but many of us have other gods such as our job or career, money, our home, the success of our children, our social standing, our physical condition, sports, golf, fishing, our car, our garden, alcohol or drugs, our position in the church or in the community, or our relationship with our friends—all of which we serve with greater fervor than we do God. For example, with respect to money, Jesus said, "No one can serve two masters, for a slave will hate the one and love the other or be devoted to one and despise the other. You cannot serve God and wealth" (Matthew 6:24). What is standing between you and God? Is there a slavery from which you need to be delivered? As you wrestle with whether to accept God, you also must wrestle with whether there is anything else you insist upon putting before God.

No matter your age or circumstances, giving up control of important parts of your life and turning those things over to an unseen God is difficult. Most of us are more comfortable with what we can see and touch and what we can accomplish through our own actions. But to test whether there is a God, at some point you must step out in faith and say you believe a power beyond yourself exists and deserves your attention. It is a wonderful thing if you can do this all at once and turn your entire life over to God, putting Him in complete control. Some people's circumstances lead them to that point, and they are blessed by it. If you are ready to do that now, *do it!* You can then skip the rest of this book, and go straight to the Bible. I suggest you start by reading any one of the four Gospels, from start to finish, and let the Lord lead you from there. But for many, transformation is not this simple. It certainly was not for me. The starting point is to believe there is a God and to state we are going to put our faith in Him.

It can be like training for a marathon: first you run a short distance—one or two miles—and then, as you train, you run farther each time until you are ready to run a twenty-six mile race. Making the decision to run the race is difficult. How will you find the time when there are so many other things you enjoy doing? Committing the time and effort to begin training also is hard, but gradually, as you continue to train for the race, you come to enjoy, and even look forward to, the running. You feel better mentally and physically as you strengthen your body. Finally, you are ready to run the race. Finishing, not winning, is the goal, and even if you do not finish, you are stronger for having tried. Putting your faith in God works in the same way. First you must commit to run the race with Him. You ask Him to guide you in a few things, and as you see Him work, you will rely on Him more and more. Your life will be enriched, and you will become stronger. You will be able to handle more pain and adversity, and joy will come from the exercise of faith and the abundance of life that comes with it.

Are you ready to take the first steps in the journey toward God? Do you want to start to learn of the mysteries, the strength, the joy and the peace that come from knowing the Lord? Something has led you to open this book and read this far. Is it your life circumstances, or the recommendation of a close friend, or an academic curiosity? It does not matter because God has led you here. Do not let other gods stand in your way. Go ahead; take the next step and turn the page.

Guiding Questions

1. Do you truly believe God exists? If so, what are the implications of that belief? How does it change your behavior or view of the world?

2. Which specific times in your life may God have been at work? Have there been any miracles in your life for which God might be responsible? If so, what are they?

3. What other "gods" do you have in your life? How do they inhibit your knowledge of and relationship with the true God?

Chapter Two

The Son

In the sixth month the angel Gabriel was sent by God to a town in Galilee called Nazareth, to a virgin engaged to a man whose name was Joseph, of the house of David. The virgin's name was Mary. And he came to her and said, "Greetings, favored one! The Lord is with you." But she was much perplexed by his words and pondered what sort of greeting this might be. The angel said to her, "Do not be afraid, Mary, for you have found favor with God. And now, you will conceive in your womb and bear a son, and you will name him Jesus. He will be great, and will be called the Son of the Most High, and the Lord God will give to him the throne of his ancestor David. He will reign over the house of Jacob forever, and of his kingdom there will be no end." Mary said to the angel,

"How can this be, since I am a virgin?" The
angel said to her, "The Holy Spirit will come
upon you, and the power of the Most High
will overshadow you; therefore the child to
be born will be holy; he will be called Son of
God. And now, your relative Elizabeth in her
old age has also conceived a son; and this is
the sixth month for her who was said to be
barren. For nothing will be impossible with
God." Then Mary said, "Here I am the servant of the Lord; let it be with me according
to your word." Then the angel departed from
her. – Luke 1:26-38

Have you ever thought about all the time and
effort you and millions of others devote to
the celebration of Christmas? We send cards; shop
for gifts; decorate our houses, offices, churches and
cities; sing carols; and attend parties. On Christmas
Eve, churches are packed with regular attendees worshipping alongside those who rarely go any other time
of year (except Easter). On Christmas morning, most
of the Christian world stands still as we exchange
gifts and celebrate with our family, friends and loved
ones on this holiest of days.

Why do we do all this? At times, in the midst
of the commotion, we are reminded to focus on the
true meaning of Christmas. Often, this is expressed
as the spirit of joyful giving symbolized by the jolly,
rotund figure called Santa Claus or Saint Nick. We
are inspired to give sacrificially at this time of year
to our friends, co-workers, neighbors, loved ones,

children, and those less fortunate than ourselves. In this process, we find joy, and we receive a glimpse of what the celebration of Christmas is supposed to be about.

But when we reflect upon the above passage from Luke or the poetic and powerful words from the beginning of the first chapter of the Gospel of John (Read John 1:1-18—"In the beginning was the Word, and the Word was with God...")—also frequently read at Christmas—we find something much greater at work than just the temporary spreading of the spirit of giving. We come to understand what should be the real reason we celebrate and worship at Christmas: God gave us the ultimate gift, his only Son. He was born of the Virgin Mary and became man in the form of Jesus Christ. "The Word became flesh and lived among us, and we have seen his glory, the glory of a father's only son, full of grace and truth" (John 1:14). This verse describes much more than the joyful, seasonal exchange of gifts. It tells us that the meaning, power and effect of the birth of Jesus Christ are far beyond the spirit and legend of Santa Claus. Santa is a great guy, but he is not Jesus.

Although you probably have celebrated Christmas each year, have you ever stopped to consider what really happened at the first Christmas? Did God, for the first and only time in history, send His Son to live among us? If you wish to take the next step in your relationship with God, this is the question with which you must wrestle. Is Jesus who He said He was—the Son of God? If you took step one, and you believe that God exists, and if you can take step two and believe that Jesus was His Son, the rest of the steps will be easy to walk, because Jesus—and those who heard His teachings and witnessed His miracles, His death and resurrection, and therefore believed in Him—will lay out a clear path for you to follow.

You may answer the question, "Do you believe in Jesus Christ?" with, "Of course I do. I am a Christian. I was baptized, and I go to church." But it is critical in taking the next steps in your relationship with the Lord to understand the impact of that response. Belief in God and in Jesus Christ as His Son is the foundation for the growth and development of a faith that will change your life. You want to be certain that foundation is strong. The goal is not a historical or academic understanding of events that occurred two thousand years ago, but rather a vibrant relationship with a living God.

These beliefs should cause you to take certain action. First and foremost, if God is God, the Creator and Supreme Ruler of the Universe and Jesus is His Son, you would be wise to learn what they say about themselves and our relationship with them by reading and studying the Bible. If God sent His only Son to live among us, don't you think He was trying to tell us something that we should be paying close attention to? God's truth, His instructions about how we are to live, is revealed in the Bible. How can this be ignored? Are you are afraid to read it? If so, why? Do you just not have enough time? If God and Jesus are who they and millions of others say they are, shouldn't you make the time? We all seem to have time to watch TV, go to movies or football games, read novels, shop, exercise, and do a myriad of other recreational activities. Do you really have a good reason not to spend time reading and seeking to understand the principal source through which God speaks to us?

Moreover, by accepting that Jesus is the Son of God, you accept that He was more than just a really good guy and a great teacher on life. You accept that He speaks the absolute truth about God and Himself, who we are, how we are to live our lives and what will happen to us when we die. Although Jesus was a teacher and prophet, in many places in Scripture, He emphasizes that He was much more:

> I am the bread of life. Whoever comes to me will never be hungry and whoever believes in me will never by thirsty. (John 6:35)

> I am the way, the truth and the life. No one comes to the Father except through me. If you know me, you will know my Father also. (John 14:6-7)

> I am the vine, and my Father is the vinegrower...I am vine, you are the branches. (John 15:1, 5)

> He gives "living water...gushing up to eternal life." (John 4:10, 14)

Jesus' claims of being "the bread of life," "living water," a "vine," and "the way and the truth and the life" are eternally profound and go much further than what a mere teacher and prophet would assert. As many have said, either Jesus was who He said He was, or He was a liar and one of the greatest con men of all time.

He's not a liar. And the truth is simple: God sent Jesus Christ, in the form of a man, so that we could know God. Jesus makes this very clear in John 14:7: "If you know me, you will know my Father also." Immediately following this statement, in John 14:8, the disciple Philip asks the same thing of Jesus that everyone on this journey has asked at some point—something you may be asking now: "Lord, show us the Father, and we will be satisfied." Note how Jesus answers him: "Have I been with you all this time and you still do not know me? Whoever has seen me has seen the Father. How can you say 'Show us the Father'? Do you not believe that I am in the Father and the Father is in me? The words that I say to you I do not speak on my own; but the Father who dwells in me does his works" (John 14: 9-10).

At this point, if you are still having trouble taking the next step and believing that Jesus is the Son of God, spend time reading the Gospel accounts of the miracles He performed. For example, Matthew 8 and 9 describe, among other miracles, His cleansing a leper (Matthew 8:1-4; see also Mark 1:40-45 and Luke 5:12-16), healing the paralyzed servant of the centurion (Matthew 8:5-13; see also Luke 7:1-10), healing a paralyzed man (Matthew 9:2-8; see also Mark 2:1-12 and Luke 5:17-26), healing a hemorrhaging woman and the apparently dead daughter of a synagogue leader (Matthew 9:18-26; see also Mark 5:21-23 and Luke 8:40-56), and giving sight to two blind men and speech to a demonic mute (Matthew 9:27-34).

The accounts of Jesus' healing miracles (and these are only a few), as well as His other miracles and those of His disciples, appear frequently throughout the New Testament. Do not take my word for it, though; read them yourself. Jesus knew the mere statement that He was the Son of God would be insufficient to convince the observers of His day (and ours) who He was. His miracles are the tangible evidence that He was the Son of God. They drew attention to Him, caused people to believe in and follow Him and spread the news about Him (remember there was no CNN).

How can we ignore these astonishing actions of Jesus? These accounts are either great fiction or they really happened. Do you believe Christianity would have grown as it has and withstood the test of two thousand years if it was based on a set of untruths and misrepresentations from a con man and his followers? We know that all Jesus' disciples, except John and Judas (who wasn't a true disciple and ended up committing suicide after betraying Jesus), were martyred for their beliefs. Would Jesus, His disciples, John the Baptist (who was beheaded), the Apostle Paul and many others have submitted to such painful deaths for a lie? Moreover, despite Jesus' crucifixion after only three years of ministry and the brutal death of his most loyal followers, the Christian faith has not only survived, but grown into the dominant religion in many parts of the world. Look around—how many churches do you see as you drive through town each day? Think about what has come out of the work of one man (albeit the Son of God) and a small band of followers who were called into service by Jesus from their very ordinary lives.

But our journey is not about religion or the numbers of people counted as Christians. We are seeking an understanding of and relationship with the Lord Himself. By coming this far, you have accepted that God exists and considered the evidence that Jesus was his Son. You may still be a bit skeptical, and you may be afraid of what a belief in God and His Son may mean and what may happen if you go on.

But do you really have much to lose by taking the next step? If God is God, and Jesus is who He said He was, can you just ignore the truth? I believe that by going forward, that is exactly what you will discover: The Truth. About God, His Son, human nature and behavior, God's will for you, how much He loves you and how He is at work in your life. We celebrate His birthday with great vigor. A vast religion bears His name. The most widely published and read book in the world is about Him and His Father.

Turn the page with me and discover the exciting truth revealed to us by God through His Son, Jesus Christ.

Guiding Questions

1. What does the celebration of Christmas mean to you?

2. How do you explain the numerous accounts in the Bible of the miracles performed by Jesus?

3. Do you regularly read the Bible? If not, what are you reading in its place? How are you currently searching for eternal truth?

Chapter Three

Come

Come to me, all you that are weary and are carrying heavy burdens, and I will give you rest. Take my yoke upon you, and learn from me; for I am gentle and humble in heart, and you will find rest for your souls. For my yoke is easy, and my burden is light.

– Matthew 11:25-28

Are you searching for something missing in your life? Are you bored or tired of your day-to-day grind? Or, are you truly depressed, suffering great pain, carrying heavy burdens for which there appears to be no hope of relief?

If these or other reasons are causing you to search for real answers to your questions, challenges and dilemmas, Jesus gives one simple answer: *Come.* In His loving arms, you will find rest for your soul, comfort from the confusion, unfairness, selfishness, and pain of this world. Allow Jesus to fill your heart with the peace, clarity, and joy that come from a personal relationship with Him.

This step is so easy. Jesus is waiting for you and saying, "Come to me just as you are." If you have already taken the first two steps of believing God exists and believing Jesus Christ is his Son, you have laid the foundation. Now, instead of looking for another job, a bigger home, a new car or spouse, or reading another self-help book, take the next step and turn to the Lord and to the Bible, the original, definitive self-help book through which the Lord is revealed.

Most of us have a good idea of how to find rest for our minds and bodies. We turn to what we know will refresh and revive us, whether it be exercise, books, movies, music, an afternoon nap, or a vacation. But what about our souls—that deep part of us, which we know is there, but do not completely understand? Is your soul restless? Can you just not seem to find peace and make yourself happy? Is your personal and family life lacking, or perhaps even in shambles? Have you achieved all the material wealth and success you sought and met all the challenges you have faced, and still cannot find meaning or peace in your life?

You may be desparate for a change. You may have experimented with drugs or alcohol or tried some other obsession like long distance running or mountain climbing. What you really may need is just a safe place to go to share, and hopefully shed your burdens. Try Jesus. He says just come and develop a relationship with Him. He will be a friend and comforter. He will help you.

Many of us are afraid to take this step. I know I was. I will never forget the trepidation I felt when I started to consider turning to Jesus for help. I did not know what it meant or what lay ahead if I chose to come to Him. What would other people, including my friends and colleagues, think if I told I them I look to Jesus for strength and guidance? Moreover, what would Jesus require of me? Would He call me to change my job, sell my house, or even become a missionary in a distant country?

You may have many of these same questions, and it is possible Jesus may require some extraordinary change in your life when you turn to Him. It is just as likely, though, He will take hold and transform you right where you are. In Matthew 11:25-28, Jesus goes to great lengths to calm your fears about turning to Him. It seems as if He already knows you are anxious about leaving the comfort and familiarity of your current situation (however good or miserable it may be) and coming to know Him. He expressly states He is "gentle and humble in heart." Despite being the Son of God, Jesus is not oppressive or overbearing. He does not have an attitude or an ego.

While your relationship with Him may, and likely will, take you places you never expected, He will gently guide and comfort you in the midst of it all. In fact, don't these words of Jesus we are examining recall the very familiar words of comfort given by David in the twenty-third psalm? "The Lord is my shepherd. I shall not want. He makes me to lie down in green pastures; he leads me beside still waters; he restores my soul. He leads me in right paths for his name's sake. Even though I walk in the darkest valley, I fear no evil; for you are with me; your rod and staff—they comfort me."

In the Matthew passage, Jesus gives a practical image of how a relationship with Him works. A key word appearing twice in these three short verses is "yoke." He says, "Take my yoke upon you," and then guarantees us, "My yoke is easy." The Webster's dictionary definition of a yoke is "a frame or a crossbar to be carried across a person's shoulders with equal loads suspended from each." It is also defined as "something that connects or joins together." As were the people of Jesus' time, we also are familiar with the yoke used with animals like oxen or mules to carry heavy loads. In invoking this image, Jesus is teaching that He is not a magician who will make our troubles, challenges and burdens suddenly disappear, but rather when we bind ourselves to Him, He provides us the means to carry the loads we could not bear otherwise.

A yoke is not a piece of equipment that will do all our work for us. It is an instrument we must choose to put on for help in performing the task at hand. At first, it looks awkward and feels uncomfortable, but as we start to carry our load, we see its benefit. We become accustomed to using it, strengthening our bodies, and less concerned about its look or feel.

We must use the yoke in the proper manner, though. When we have completed our task, we come to admire its simplicity and understand we would not want to meet the challenge of that task again without the yoke. And the more we use it, we become stronger and more proficient, able to accomplish even greater tasks.

The comparison to Jesus should be obvious. At first, the reliance on Him is awkward and uncomfortable. We wish we were strong enough to do it on our own. We fear what people will think. Like someone who comes to rely on the yoke to carry a heavy load, however, it is wise to use an available tool to ease our burden, even if it looks odd and is unfamiliar initially. In the long run, we are better off having relied upon it, rather than allowing a difficult load to eventually wear us down.

Therefore, come quiet your soul and find rest in Jesus Christ. Take up the yoke of the Lord and depend on Him. This step is easy.

Take it.

Guiding Questions

1. How do you find rest for your soul?

2. What would you like to change in your life?

3. Is something keeping you from turning to Jesus for comfort and relief? If so, what is it and why can't you let go of it?

Chapter Four

Be Transformed

Do not be conformed to this world, but be transformed by the renewing of your mind, so that you may discern what is the will of God—what is good and acceptable and perfect. – Romans 12:2

The last step you took was to come to Christ, and once He is in your life, everything will be different. You will begin to see and understand things you never did before. Paul tells us in 2 Corinthians 6:17: "If anyone is in Christ, there is a new creation: everything old has passed away; see, everything has become new." A new light will be shed upon all that is around you.

Remember those familiar words from the first chapter of John's Gospel: "What has come into being in him was life, and the life was the light of all people. That light shines in the darkness and the darkness did not overcome it" (John 1:3-4). As the light of Jesus Christ begins to shine into your life, your mind, heart and spirit will begin a transformation. You will come to recognize that God's and the world's perspectives are radically different. Passages from the Bible, novels, poems, movies, TV shows and the behavior of certain people will suddenly make sense, where before they were confounding or mysterious.

For much of your life, you likely have viewed yourself solely from an earthly and human perspective. Since we were very young, many of us were encouraged to be popular, look out for ourselves, succeed, accumulate wealth and seek recognition for our accomplishments. But Jesus teaches us something completely different. In Luke 14:11, He warns, "For all who exalt themselves will be humbled, and those who humble themselves will be exalted," and in Matthew 16:25, He counsels, "For those who want to save their life will lose it..." (See also Mark 8:35, Luke 9:24 and the next chapter.)

You may have heard these or other passages before and been confused. You may have even ignored them as contrary to what your parents, coaches or teachers had taught you. Now the truth will be revealed to you, though, and these passages will begin to make sense.

Please understand, I am *not* saying you will suddenly have life all figured out or everything will start going your way because you have received the Lord. Making Jesus a part of your life is merely the first step in a lifelong journey. You (and I) will never have it all under control or (for you compulsive overachievers) graduate to the head of some elite class where you will be recognized as a superior Christian. A life of transforming faith will instead move you from a reliance on yourself to a reliance on God. You will no longer believe in what you can see or control, but rather in what you cannot see or control.

The step of giving up control—which I will address in greater detail in the next chapter—is closely linked to the step of renewal and transformation. I believe that once you have taken these two steps, you will have passed a great turning point in your spiritual journey, and your life truly will be changed.

The Apostle Paul, who wrote the Book of Romans and knew something about transformation and giving up control (see the story of his Damascus Road experience in Acts 22:6-16), is telling us in Romans 12:2 about one principal way to be transformed: by renewing your mind; therefore, the next step I challenge you to take is to commit to transformation. You must change your perspective from a worldly view, based on your own desires and the desires of those who may influence you, to a Godly view, based on faith in the Lord. Something must have inspired you to take the last step and come to the loving arms of Jesus and take His yoke upon you. What was it? Were you seeking some kind of change? If so, now is the point at which you must implement that change by actively committing to transformation and renewal. You must realize you are a new creation, and act accordingly. You must actually cease contemplating how the yoke may work and go ahead and pick it up. You must move on with the business of life, assuming its daily responsibilities, with the Lord now at your side showing you the way. In doing so, you will discover what Paul tells us is one of the inspiring results of transformation and renewal: discerning the will of God.

The good news is you do not have to do any of this alone. From the moment you told God "I believe," He gave you strength to act through the power of the Holy Spirit who is now living in you. You must learn to rely upon the Holy Spirit as opposed to only your own instincts and experience, which can lead you astray. In Mark 1:8, John the Baptist says of Jesus, "I will baptize you with water; but he will baptize you with the Holy Spirit." Then Jesus Himself tells His disciples in John 14:25-27:

> I have said these things to you while I am still with you. But the Advocate, the Holy Spirit, whom the Father will send in my name, will teach you everything, and remind you of all that I have said to you. Peace I leave with you; my peace I give to you. I do not give to you as the world gives. Do not let your hearts be troubled, and do not let them be afraid.

With the presence of the Holy Spirit, we each have an interior guidance system from the Lord, directing our transformation. The Spirit of God, the third member of the Trinity, and His power is loaded into us, like new software into a computer. Step by step, we will gradually come to recognize and obey the Holy Spirit, desiring to become increasingly and—by the grace of God—totally reliant on Him.

This requires believing in the power of God, which you rarely see or touch, but experience and obey. As Jesus told Nicodemus in John 3:8: "The wind blows where it chooses, and you hear the sound of it, but you do not know where it comes from or where it goes. So it is with everyone who is born of the Spirit." Jesus also stated to Thomas—one of the twelve disciples (known as "Doubting Thomas")—when He appeared to him and the other disciples following His resurrection: "Have you believed because you have seen me? Blessed are those who have not seen and yet have come to believe" (John 20:26).

As you begin to seek God's will over your own, the evidence of His hand upon your life will be revealed. You will reprioritize. Your relationships with your family and friends will change. You will spend your time and your money differently. You will do things you never thought you would. You will stop worrying about what other people think of you and your actions and start paying attention to what God thinks and to where He is leading you. At first, you may be uncomfortable and even afraid, but Jesus tells us:

> Do not worry about your life, what you will eat or what you will drink, or about your body, what you will wear...indeed your heavenly Father knows that you need all these things. But strive first for the kingdom of God and

his righteousness, and all these things will be given to you as well. (Matthew 6:25, 32-33)

When we focus on our relationship with God and the discernment of and obedience to His will, making those our first priorities, everything else falls into place. Our fears, concerns and anxieties will be transformed into peace, patience, and confidence in the Lord and where He is taking us.

We also are not alone as we have the Word of God to show us the way. You may think what I have been describing so far about developing a relationship with the Lord has been a bit abstract, so I want to give you a few practical suggestions. The first is simple: read the Bible. In fact, it is more than a suggestion, it is an imperative. The Bible is the absolute source of truth about God, Jesus, the Holy Spirit, prayer, sacrifice, obedience, love and everything else about how God wants us, His children, to live our lives. I am confident as you read, study and reflect upon this holy book, you will begin to understand the eternal truths revealed inside.

Don't you wish your parents had given you a book answering the difficult questions in life to guide you as you finally left home? That's exactly what our heavenly Father and Creator of the world we live in did. But you must study it consistently. You simply cannot go further in your journey with the Lord without committing to read and study His instruction manual. You should schedule time each day to choose a Bible passage and reflect upon what it means to you. You will not regret it. Just like with a piece of complex machinery, the more thoroughly you study the instructions, the easier it will be to use and the more you will get out of it.

The Bible is alive with the remarkable truth of God, our Creator. John 1:1 tells us: "In the beginning was the Word, and the Word was with God, and the Word was God." John 1:14 states, "And the Word became flesh and lived among us, and we have seen his glory, and the glory as of a father's only son, full of grace and truth." I believe the search for God is also the search for Truth. God's Word is Truth. We have the opportunity to discover what is real and true and what really works. Through Jesus, God reveals to us His truth and lets us know what He expects of us as His children. Jesus says in John 8:31 and 32: "If you continue in my word, you are truly my disciples, and you will know the truth, and the truth will make you free."

Jesus is a friend, companion, and teacher. The more time you spend with Him and studying the Word of God revealed through Him, the stronger your knowledge of and relationship with Jesus and the Father becomes. Is this not true of any teacher or friend? If you do not go to class or open the textbook, you will not learn much about the subject being taught. If you never call, write or spend time with a friend, your friendship will fade away. I know you are busy (I am, too), but you have to make time for being with God and reading the Bible in a way that works for you. You may want to find a daily devotional book that gives you some structure and insight into your reading (this is how I began and is still the method I use), or you may just want to read one of the Gospels or other books of the Bible from beginning to end.

Following Jesus' command, "But strive first for the kingdom of God..." (Matthew 6:33), I try to start each day spending time reading the Bible and in prayer. A remarkable transformation occurred when I began this discipline. Each day seems to go more smoothly when I begin focused on the Lord and allow the Holy Spirit, rather than my personal desires, to control my agenda. Conversely, the days I do not begin with the Lord are more chaotic and less productive. As with tithing—the concept of giving God the first fruits of your labor and income—you should give God your best time, not what is left over after you have done everything else you wanted to do.

But this is merely the beginning. You also can participate in a Bible study; listen to sermons or instruction on CDs, online and on the radio; watch preachers on TV or video; or go on a retreat with your church or another group committed to helping you grow your knowledge of and relationship with the Lord. Joining a group study, for example, is helpful because you not only hear how the Holy Spirit is teaching and guiding others, but you hold one another accountable as you meet challenges together in your walk with the Lord. You will feel blessed as God connects you with countless others on the same journey, opening you to a reservoir of bountiful resources you never knew existed. Just like asking directions at the service station when you are lost on a trip, it helps if you rely on people who have some idea of the way ahead to give you direction. Again, no one has it all figured out, but many possess wisdom, experience, and the desire to assist you.

As wonderful as that assistance from wise people is, though, it won't take you all the way in your walk with God. You need to communicate directly with the all-wise, all-knowing Creator of the Universe. This is done through prayer—a discipline vital to the transformation and renewing of our minds. As Romans 12:2 tells us, we are struggling not to conform to this world, but rather to transform ourselves by the renewing of our minds for one purpose: "so that we may discern what is the will of God."

We are seeking to know and understand not what we want in and from this world, but what God wants us to do in it. Using the Holy Spirit at work within us, we need to discern God's will for us. What is He working out in the world around us? What is it He wants us to do for Him at this moment? While there are times we must concern ourselves with long-term decisions, in prayer there is great benefit in focusing on the immediate moment.

As Jesus advises in Matthew 6:34, the verse directly following the one about seeking first the kingdom of God: "So do not worry about tomorrow, for tomorrow will bring worries of its own. Today's trouble is enough for today." Prayer is the principal way God reveals His will to us, and prayer in this context is not so much an exercise in speaking to God, but rather in listening to Him.

Take the time to clear your mind of everything else, and just listen for the Lord. He may or may not speak to you directly. I have heard many people talk of direct encounters and conversations with the Lord. Others describe being gently nudged along by Him. He speaks to different people in different ways, but if you listen closely and watch for Him, you will see His hand at work in your life and in the lives of others. Be guided by Him, but remember, you are listening not for what you want, but rather for what He wants—His will, which very well may be much different from what you were expecting (see Isaiah 55:8: "My thoughts are not your thoughts neither are your ways my ways, says the Lord."). Be certain you are paying close attention or you may miss what He provides in answer to your prayer. I know this has been particularly true in my role as a parent. God often has provided answers to my prayers for my children, which are far different, and better, then what I thought they needed.

You must renew your mind so you can discern the will of God and what He is doing in and through you. It is His will that is good, acceptable and perfect. Your will is always flawed. Once you discern His will, your life will be transformed in miraculous ways. One warning: Do not confuse discerning the will of God and being obedient to what you discern with knowing and understanding how God works. You will never fully understand in this world how and why certain things happen and why God works the way he does. Although this is often your first inclination, do not waste time and energy on it. His knowledge and wisdom are infinitely beyond all of us. As Paul describes in 1 Corinthians 13:12: "For now we see in a mirror, dimly, but then we will see face to face. Now I know only in part; then I will know fully, even as I have been fully known." Just gaze upon and ponder the beauty of creation or the complexity of the natural processes of our universe, which no human being could have designed. At best, you will only get a vague glimpse of how God works in this world. But that's okay, because He is the one in control. And He is good.

I hope as you consider the truths we discussed in this chapter and the preceding chapters about the reality of God and His Son that you are trusting Jesus for help and comfort and allowing the Holy Spirit and the Word of God to refresh you, renew your mind, change your perspective, and reveal to you His will. And with God's grace, you are prepared for the next vital step in your journey: giving up control of your life to the One who is in control of *all* life.

Guiding Questions

1. What, if anything, in your life looks different to you as you have begun to view it from God's perspective?

2. What steps could you take at this point to strengthen your faith and renew your mind? Join a small group or Bible study? Go on a retreat? Meet and talk with someone who you know believes in Jesus Christ?

3. Is there a time each day you could set aside to pray and listen to God? If so, when? If not, is there something you could sacrifice in order to make time for God?

Chapter Five

Give Up Control

Then Jesus told his disciples, "If any want to become my followers, let them deny themselves and take up their cross and follow me. For those who want to save their life will lose it, and those who lose their life for my sake will find it. For what will it profit them if they gain the whole world, but forfeit their life? Or what will they give in return for their life?" – Matthew 16:25-26 (See also Mark 8:34-36 and Luke 9:23-25.)

Jesus seems to be making a paradoxical statement in this passage. He says if we want to save our life, we will lose it; but if we lose it, we will find it. How do we make sense of this? Surely He is not telling us to submit to a physical death so we can get to heaven and find our life there. Is He telling everyone to completely change the life they are leading and do something radically different? He certainly seems to be telling us the opposite of everything popular culture teaches us: to "go for it," accumulate as much wealth and power as you can, climb to the top and be number one.

We are at a critical point in our journey, and I ask you to read and consider these passages very carefully. Note the text is almost identical in the three referenced Gospels. The inclusion of these verses by all three authors underscores the truth, wisdom and importance of this passage. As discussed in the previous chapter, the steps of being transformed, discerning the will of God and giving up control or of "losing" your life are vital turning points in your journey with the Lord.

Jesus is telling us in these verses what we need to do if we want to be one of His followers. It is significant that He begins by stating, "If any want to become my followers..." (no exceptions—including you) and then proceeds with a requirement that is anything but an easy, warm-up step. He demands that we deny ourselves, take up His cross (not our own) and follow Him. Instead of telling us to follow our own instincts and common sense, He commands complete surrender, which does not come naturally to any of us.

Is this the way one rounds up people to be followers of the world's next great religion? Today, we may expect to start a spiritual life with something a little easier, like singing in the choir or going to a Sunday school class. But complete surrender was Jesus' demand of the first believers who were to be the foundation of Christianity. Why should we expect to give any less if we are to have a meaningful, intimate relationship with Him today?

When I first read these verses, I was confounded as to their meaning. But once I really began to put my faith in the Lord, they started to make sense. This is why the steps in the preceding chapters are so essential. Taking this step is not possible if you do not believe that God is God, that Jesus is his Son, that you need to look to Him for comfort and guidance, and that He can transform your life. If you are at the point where you are ready to trade your existing life for a new one, this step will come more easily. But the more you want to hold on to what you have, the harder it will be to let go when the Lord asks you to. Jesus told His disciples following His conversation with the rich young ruler, "it is easier for a camel to go through the eye of a needle than for someone who is rich to enter the kingdom of heaven" (Mark 10:26). He then addresses their concern about the harshness of such a statement by assuring them that "for God all things are possible" (Mark 10:27).

If you can take this step and meet the demands Jesus makes in these verses, there will be a great turning point in your journey, changing you forever. If you are willing to let go and lose your life for His sake, you will find a life richer and more abundant than you ever imagined, regardless of whether you think you are satisfied with the one you already have.

The issue Jesus addresses in these verses is perhaps the central issue in anyone's faith journey: control. Who or what is in control of your life? Is it your job or career? Your desire for money or financial security? Your drive to be the best? Your friends? The success of your children? What others think of you? Your physical condition or appearance? Your material possessions? Drugs or alcohol? Are you controlled by earlier events in your life that continue to influence you, such as the death of a loved one, a troubled childhood, divorce or financial failure? Are you obsessed with controlling the actions of your family or those who work with you? How much anxiety or wasted time and energy are generated by your concern about these things?

While it is challenging for each of us to give up control of our lives, what makes it so much easier is the realization that Jesus Christ died for us on the Cross. He was the perfect sacrifice for our sins. There is nothing else we need to do to earn God's love, and therefore nothing else we need to control. Simply believing in Him and His Son, Jesus, brings His grace and favor. In Romans 3:24-25, the Apostle Paul put it this way: "Since all have sinned and fall short of the glory of God, they are now justified by his grace as a gift, through the redemption that is in Jesus Christ, whom God put forward as a sacrifice of atonement by his blood, effective through faith."

When you lack control over something you care deeply about, you feel weak and powerless, and therefore are anxious; but Paul, when speaking of a particular weakness of his own in 2 Corinthians 12:9, tells us the Lord told him, "My grace is sufficient for you, for power is made perfect in weakness."

Therefore, you should strive to give God control of everything and everyone you feel compelled to control. To save your life, lose it. Let go. Let Jesus guide, direct, comfort, heal and support you. Let your life be about His business, not yours—not just in some things, but in everything. Stop thinking about what you can get out of life, and start following and obeying God.

As you begin to let go of your own desires, ambitions and goals, and follow those set out for you by God, you will be transformed. Your stress level will go down. You will be at peace with yourself and others around you. Your use of time and resources will become more fruitful. Your understanding of God's will for you will become much clearer as the Holy Spirit takes over. You will discover relationships, opportunities and blessings you never thought possible.

I have been blessed to serve in a number of leadership positions over the years. Some of these were positions coveted by others. I can truly tell you, however, I never sought or coveted a single one. In fact, in some instances, I was very reluctant to take on the responsibilities asked of me. In almost every case, though, I was blessed by the experience because God was ultimately using me to do His work, for His purposes, not mine. Conversely, I have declined many attractive opportunities by following the Lord's will and not my own.

Please understand, however, that when I was not listening to the Lord, I made my share of poor decisions, committing to obligations that I later regretted, while turning down those perhaps I should have pursued. As we discussed in the previous chapter, the key is discerning the will of God through Scripture, prayer and fellowship with and counsel from other believers.

You should begin to put each day in God's hands and cease striving to control the events and details of your life. This likely will be a daily struggle. Please note I have said you are at a turning point in the journey, not the end. In many ways, the decision to give up control of your life is only the beginning. It is like mountain climbing. You spend a significant amount of time in preparation before you ever take the first step; and then you still have the entire trek before you. Each step will be a struggle, but you are exhilarated by the challenge and determined to reach the ultimate goal.

Denying yourself, taking up your cross and losing your life for Jesus' sake will be a challenge, but the exercising of your faith and the resulting sacrifice of yourself and your desires is like training to climb that mountain. Very few will just show up and climb without any preparation. Most begin by studying and organizing, and then pursue their training by going shorter distances and working up to the point where they can go the entire way.

You may want to begin by exercising your faith in smaller things and work up to turning more and more over to God. Spend a few minutes in prayer and Bible reading at the beginning of each day. If you pay attention, you should find you are less anxious and more fruitful over the course of the day.

Increase your giving to your church or any other cause through which lives are being changed for the glory of God. You will experience a transformation in your own life as a result. Listen to what God is telling you about what your spouse, children or other members of your family should be doing. It may be very different from your own vision, which is subject to limited experience and selfish desires. Now that you have another source of wisdom and guidance, though, rely on it. God will direct you appropriately.

It is possible, though, that your current circumstances may require you to take not small steps, but a giant leap of faith. If so, do not hesitate. You may be fighting serious illness, severe depression, crippling addiction, loss of a loved one or a financial crisis and need immediate relief. It may be that you must start climbing the mountain right now. If so, put yourself in God's hands and He will guide and comfort you.

One thing you cannot compromise is to surrender your entire life to Jesus. There can be no question regarding your commitment to the journey and where it will lead you. The only unknowns—based on your personal circumstances—are the size of the steps and the pace at which you progress. Rarely are you given a clear road map as to precisely where you are headed. It is a lifelong growth process. You will be required to exercise your faith and become increasingly dependent upon an unseen Lord. As John the Baptist told his followers: "He must increase, but I must decrease" (John 3:30).

You also cannot turn only portions of our life over to the Lord. Hedging your bets by keeping control of some things (such as work or finances), but turning others over to Jesus (such as healing a loved one) will not succeed. Many have used the metaphor of how you treat a guest in your home. If the guest is a close friend, you will not restrict him to certain parts of your home, but will make him fully welcome in all the rooms. You often will tell such a friend to "make themselves at home." Are you willing to do that with Jesus, letting Him in all the rooms of your home?

Believing in, coming to and following Jesus in totality requires you to change the way you view the world. Do not be afraid to listen to what God wants and let go of what you want. He has in store for you a life much fuller, richer and better than the one you have mapped out for yourself. Paraphrasing Jesus, he tells us, "Lose your life, and you will find a better one. Struggle to hold on to the one you have against the will of God, and you will continue to be discontent and unfulfilled."

How many selfish, greedy, egotistical people do you know at peace with themselves? How often do you see someone who has achieved significant worldly success, but has sacrificed their marriage or their relationship with their children or other family members along the way? Despite what you may think, you have little control over the events of your life. The plan you have crafted for yourself can be significantly altered by illness, addiction, death, change in economic conditions, natural calamity or a variety of other factors. God's plan for you is based on His truth and His love for you. As Moses told the Israelites: "it is the Lord your God who goes with you; he will not fail you or forsake you" (Deuteronomy 31:5).

The best explanation I have ever heard or read of this principle is from C. S. Lewis in his classic, *Mere Christianity*. He concluded the book eloquently and profoundly, by stating:

> ... there must be a real giving up of self. You must throw it away 'blindly' so to speak. Christ will indeed give you a real personality: but you must not go to Him for the sake of that. As long as your own personality is what you are bothering about you are not going to Him at all. The very first step is to try to forget about the self altogether. Your real, new self (which is Christ's and also yours, and yours just because it is His) will not come as long as you are looking for Him. Does that sound strange? The same principle holds, you know, for more everyday matters. Even in social life, you will never make a good impression on other people until you stop thinking about what sort of impression you are making. Even in literature and art, no man who bothers about originality will ever be original: whereas if you simply try to tell the truth (without caring twopence how often it has been told before) you will, nine times out of ten, become original without ever having noticed it. The principle runs through all life from top to bottom. Give up yourself, and you will find your real self. Lose your life

and you will save it. Submit to death, death of your ambitions and favorite wishes every day and death of your whole body in the end: submit with every fiber of your being, and you will find eternal life. Keep nothing back. Nothing that you have not given away will be really yours. Nothing in you that has not died will ever be raised from the dead. Look for yourself, and you will find in the long run only hatred, loneliness, despair, rage, ruin and decay. But look for Christ and you will find Him, and with Him everything else thrown in.[1]

---

[1] C. S. Lewis, *Mere Christianity* (1952, HarpersCollins Edition 2001), page 226-227.

Guiding Questions

1. What is the most important thing to you in your life? Does it control you, and if so, how?

2. Are there areas of your life you are unwilling to turn over to the Lord? Why?

3. What or whom are you trying to control? Would it be better if you turned control of those matters or people over to the Lord? What might that look like?

Chapter Six

Abide

I am the true vine, and my Father is the vine-grower. He removes every branch in me that bears no fruit. Every branch that bears fruit he prunes to make it bear more fruit. You have already been cleansed by the word that I have spoken to you. Abide in me as I abide in you. Just as the branch cannot bear fruit by itself unless it abides in the vine, neither can you unless you abide in me. I am the vine, you are the branches. Those who abide in me and I in them bear much fruit, because apart from me you can do nothing. Whoever does not abide in me is thrown away like a branch and withers; such branches are gathered, thrown into the fire and burned. If you abide in me, and my words abide in you, ask whatever you wish, and it will be done for you. My Father is glorified by this, that you bear much fruit and

become my disciples. As the Father has loved me, so I have loved you; abide in my love. If you keep my commandments, you will abide in my love, just as I have kept my Father's commandments and abide in his love. I have said these things to you, so that my joy may be in you, and that your joy may be complete.
– John 15:1-12

Once you find the faith and the will to give up control of your life, you will be prepared to take the next crucial step in your journey, which will not only provide the strength and power to continue to release control, but also will help you develop a permanent bond with the Lord. You must abide in Him and let Him abide in you. Isn't this what you really want—a solid, continuing condition of faith allowing you to relinquish your dependence on worldly relationships and things to instead enjoy deep communion with the true, faithful and loving God who created you?

In the John 15 passage, Jesus provides a powerful image of the way our relationship with the Father, Son, and Holy Spirit works. The metaphors Jesus uses are among the most vivid and profound in the Bible. He compares us to the branch of a vine (visualize a grapevine—which was common in the area Jesus lived and preached—or almost any similar fruit-bearing tree or plant). He tells us what we know to be true: a branch cannot bear fruit by itself, and, cut off from the vine, eventually withers and dies. Without its connection to the living vine, it has no possible source of life, and it is "gathered, thrown into the fire, and burned" (John 15:6).

Think about this—not only does the branch die, but also its fruit, flowers and leaves. A branch connected to the vine, however, is alive, flourishing and producing fruit. Nutrients come through the roots, into the vine and to the branch and its leaves and fruit. Sunlight is absorbed by the leaves and flows back through the branch and to the vine. The whole process works in harmony to produce a healthy and productive plant. The branch abides in the vine, and the vine in the branch.

Jesus tells us that our relationship with Him is to work in the same way. He says, "Abide in me as I abide in you. Just as the branch cannot bear fruit by itself unless it abides in the vine, neither can you unless you abide in me" (John 15:4). Our relationship with Jesus is a two-way relationship. Isn't it true that any loving relationship—whether marriage, friendship, family, a community, a business, an orchestra or a basketball team—is stronger when all parties are actively communicating and sacrificing for each other and for the good of the whole? Look at what Jesus says about those who are connected to the vine: "Those who abide in me and I in them bear much fruit" (John 15:5). "If you abide in me, and my words abide in you, ask for whatever you wish, and it will be done for you" (John 15:7).

By contrast, observe what Jesus says about those who do not have a relationship with Him: "Whoever does not abide in me is thrown away like a branch and withers" (John 15:6). Consider the image of a branch ripped away from a tree, plant or vine: nothing can be done to bring it to life. It cannot bear fruit, and it eventually does wither, die and is of no use other than to be thrown into the fire.

This is true of our lives when we are not connected to the Lord. We are not productive and do not bear fruit as we should. Often the effect is gradual, like a withering branch. Slowly we become self-absorbed, our relationships deteriorate and our productivity evaporates, like rotting branches and dying leaves decomposing into the soil. How many marriages have you seen disintegrate over many years until they eventually wither and die in divorce? Consider those you know who have been addicted to drugs, alcohol or their work, or otherwise have allowed worldly matters to divert them from their relationships with their families and loved ones to the point where their relationships are decayed and dying. Conversely, if we abide in Jesus, we find the strength and will to follow the right course and avoid harmful and destructive behavior. Jesus states, "apart from me you can do nothing" (John 15:6). Given the incredible promises of these verses, why choose to try to do anything on your own without an abiding relationship with Jesus?

One important distinction in these verses is the difference between the withered branch disconnected from the vine and the branch that is pruned, but remains connected to the vine. In John 15:2, Jesus states, "Every branch that bears fruit he prunes to make it bear more fruit." Here Jesus is addressing the role of painful change in the life of a believer.

Make no mistake; there will be change in your life, and it very well may be unexpected and painful (or at least uncomfortable). It may be illness or death of a friend or loved one, a change in employment or residence, financial loss, natural calamity or any one of a number of other life-changing events. Jesus is telling you that as long you stay connected to Him, you will not only survive, but ultimately you will be made stronger and more fruitful by your challenges. This is exactly what happens when one prunes the branch of a vine. It is painful and unsightly at first, but ultimately the branch and the vine grow stronger and produce more leaves, flowers and fruit.

It is important to recognize that, despite the steps set forth in this book, or others you plan for yourself, this pruning may occur at any time. You must be prepared, understanding that your response to a pruning event is a vital step in your journey with the Lord (consider it a detour), and that the only response guaranteed to strengthen you is to remain connected to Him. As a result, your life and strength come almost exclusively from the vine (Christ). And as you continue to receive that strength by abiding in Him, like the pruned branch, you gradually will grow and flourish.

As I mentioned before, I have experienced such "pruning events," some severe and painful, and some even leading me to question how God could possibly allow such a thing to take place. But He has sustained me through all those times, despite my doubts, and as a result of each, I emerged stronger, more faithful, more joyful and bearing more fruit for His glory.

You also should pay attention to the vinegrower (or gardener) in this passage. Jesus tells us that while He is the vine to which we are connected, God is the vinegrower (John 15:1). It is God who removes every branch bearing no fruit and prunes the branches that do. You also can assume it is He who does the planting, watering, fertilizing, weeding and harvesting. He is actively doing good things for you, which will allow you to grow, strengthen and bear fruit for Him. You are called only to obey and be content to serve as the branch bearing the harvest for God.

Also consider the fruit is harvested by the gardener for the gardener's purposes. The branch itself has no choice as to its function for the vine. And eventually, the branch must let go of its fruit, for it belongs to the gardener, who picks it from the branch.

When you abide in Christ and allow him to abide in you, you are better able to obey God's will. He will meet all your needs in order to carry out that will. There is no reason for anxiety. There is a great peace and joy in simply serving as a branch resting on the vine as you receive nourishment and bear the fruit God will pick and use for His purposes. In Matthew 6:25-27, Jesus says,

> ...do not worry about your life, what you will eat or what you will drink, or about your body, what you will wear. Is not life more than food and the body more than clothing? Look at the birds of the air; they neither sow nor reap nor gather into barns, and yet your

heavenly Father feeds them. Are you not of more value than they?

If you stay connected to the Lord, He promises to care for you.

In his excellent book on this topic, *Abide in Christ*, Andrew Murray explains that abiding in Christ is not optional, but rather a command. A command, however, full of grace and love, which, if followed, will lead us to a more complete relationship with the Lord. Note this in the following passage from *Abide in Christ*, and also note the connection Murray draws between the John 15:1-12 passage we are examining in this chapter and Matthew 11:25-28 ("Come to me..."), which we addressed in Chapter Three:

> The blessings He bestows are all connected with His "Come to me," and are only to be enjoyed in close fellowship with Himself. You either did not fully understand, or did not rightly remember, that the call meant, "Come *to me* to stay with *me*." And yet this was in very deed His object and purpose when He first called you to Himself. It was not to refresh you for a few short hours after your conversion with the joy of His love and deliverance, and then to send you forth to wander in sadness and sin. He had destined you to something better than short-lived blessedness, to be enjoyed only in times of special earnestness and prayer, and then to pass away,

as you had to return to those duties in which far the greater part of life has to be spent. No, indeed; He had prepared for you an abiding dwelling with Himself, where your whole life and every moment of it might be spent, where the work of your daily life might be done, and where all the while you might be enjoying unbroken communion with Himself. It was even this he meant when to that first word, "Come to me," He added this "Abide in me." As earnest and faithful, as loving and tender, as the compassion that breathed in that blessed "Come," was the grace that added this no less blessed "Abide." As mighty as the attraction with which the first word drew you, were the bonds with which this second, had you listened to it, would have kept you. And as great as were the blessings with which that coming was rewarded, so large, yea, and much greater, were the treasures to which that abiding would have given you access.[2]

Perhaps due to the image of the vine and the branch given by Jesus, the act of abiding in Christ and allowing Him to abide in you may be becoming easier to conceptualize, but it remains among the most difficult steps to implement. It is directly related to and complimentary of the step of giving up control. Letting go becomes easier as you begin to permanently bind yourself to and rely upon Christ

---

[2] Andrew Murray, *Abide in Christ* (1979, Whitaker House), page 12.

and His love. You begin to work toward a permanent condition of faith in God through Christ where you are sustained and strengthened by Christ and the Holy Spirit. You trade the illusive happiness of this world for the complete joy that will be delivered by an abiding relationship with Jesus Christ. This step is a great turning point in your journey with the Lord because you are committing to making your relationship with Him permanent. You are asking Him to sustain you, rather than be sustained by your worldly abilities, successes, possessions or relationships, which even in the best of circumstances will fail you.

One way to look at it is that before now you were just "dating," but now you are "getting married." Previously you had fleeting, occasional contact with the Lord. You probably celebrated Christmas and Easter. You may have gone to church and Sunday school most Sundays. Perhaps you even went to a Bible study or prayed to God when you needed something. But now, like a marriage, the step you are taking is your decision to make your relationship with Jesus Christ permanent. You are collapsing the walls that prevented a complete dependence on the Lord and deciding to create a lasting bond that will sustain you from this day forward. This is not a decision you make wholly unto yourself, but rather you are guided by the Holy Spirit. Each day, each hour, and even each minute, you are called to abide in Him and work to establish a free-flowing connection to Him, which will allow the Holy Spirit—rather than your own wants and desires—to direct you. Isn't this what you really want—to fill the voids in your life with a closer, more loving relationship with Christ, where you are understood fully, loved unconditionally and sustained by the one who created you and cares deeply about you?

Abiding in Jesus Christ and His abiding in you will not occur instantly. Cementing your relationship with and dependence upon Him is a lifelong process, but you can begin today to follow His command to abide, then work each day thereafter to nourish and strengthen that bond through reading and studying the Bible and other sources (try C.S. Lewis, Andrew Murray, John Stott (*Basic Christianity)* or one of the many other great Christian writers), as well as through prayer, worship, fellowship, sacrificial service and giving, and whatever other means God calls you to.

This process will not follow a linear upward progression by which you systematically strengthen your relationship with the Lord. Life does not work that way. While I truly believe your peace, joy and inner strength will grow, there will be times of struggle, trial, disappointment, loss and failure, where God seems distant and your connection to Him weakened. You should recognize these as times of pruning where by resting firmly in the grace and love of God you ultimately will come through with a stronger bond to Christ (the vine), our heavenly Father (the gardener) and the Holy Spirit (a life-sustaining source of nourishment and strength). Remember, a branch cannot bear fruit unless it is connected to the vine.

So begin today—by abiding in Jesus and allowing Him to abide in you with the hope that Christ's "joy may be in you and your joy may be complete" (John 15:12). Then you will be prepared for the steps to come, including the next one, where you will need to take up your cross and be crucified with Christ.

Are you ready?

Guiding Questions

1. What are your sources of nourishment that strengthen your bond to the Lord? How can you increase the flow of these to strengthen that bond?

2. What have been some of the most painful and challenging times in your life? How have these been times of "pruning?" What growth has resulted from them?

3. What do you worry about? Can you release your worries to the Lord? If not, why not?

Chapter Seven

Crucified with Christ

"I have been crucified with Christ and it is no longer I who live, but it is Christ who lives in me. And the life I now live in the flesh I live by faith in the Son of God who loved me and gave himself for me." — Galatians 2:19-20

The Apostle Paul's reference in this passage to being crucified with Christ may seem extreme. You may question how it could ever apply to you. The essence of Paul's message, however, is easy to understand; it is the implementation that is difficult. To put it simply, your ego has to go. Not just some, but all of it. It has to be sacrificed on the cross with Christ, where He sacrificed Himself for us. Yes, your ego: your image of yourself, your individuality, your vision of who you are and what you will become— which you may have spent so much time, effort, and perhaps money, creating—must be sacrificed on the cross.

This may run contrary to what you have been taught to this point in your life, because the world bombards us with the opposite message: achieve as much as you can, be famous, be wealthy, seek recognition, build your resume, and celebrate yourself and your accomplishments. But rejecting this and instead being crucified with Christ is absolutely vital to the continued growth in your relationship with the Lord, for this is the heart of the Christian message: in death there is new life. After Jesus' suffering and dying, he was resurrected. There must be Good Friday so there can be Easter. This is why we frequently see references to John 3:16, which captures the essence of the Christian faith: "For God so loved the world that he gave his only Son, so that everyone who believes in him may not perish but have eternal life."

Just as Jesus was crucified and rose again on the third day, when you crucify your own individuality and ego on the cross, God will give you a new, fuller and better life in Jesus Christ. You will never experience all God has to offer until you completely sacrifice your right to your self.

Being crucified with Christ, however, requires more than just unselfishness and doing good deeds. You must be prepared to make a wholesale change, which is a daily challenge for even the most committed believer. Think of it as if you were performing a substantial renovation of your home. You must be prepared to move out many of your interests, needs and desires (your own individuality) to make room for what God through Christ is going to move In. The Holy Spirit needs a lot of space to operate in order to make room for what God has planned for you and wants to teach you. Like renovating your home, it will take time; and with God's help, you may have to painstakingly move out each thought and desire piece by piece, like furniture, then knock down walls, rearrange windows and doors, repaint and install new fixtures. You must be fully prepared to allow God to empty you and recreate you in His image. The result will be the home will have essentially the same skeletal structure, but will be new, fresh and different.

One of the great examples of how to take this step was John the Baptist, who many thought was the Messiah. Matthew 3:5 tells us: "Then the people of Jerusalem were going out to him, and all the region along the Jordan, and they were baptized by him in the river Jordan, confessing their sins." John had become very popular, and he easily could have allowed his own popularity to fuel his ego and cloud his understanding of his true role. Yet he knew he was not the Messiah, but rather the one who was to prepare the way for the Messiah. John 1:6-9 tells us: "There was a man sent from God, whose name was John. He came as a witness to testify to the light, so that all might believe through him. He himself was not the light, but came to testify to the light. The true light, which enlightens everyone, was coming into the world."

When people began to flock to Jesus to be baptized, instead of to John the Baptist, John's disciples asked him about this new teacher. We can speculate they were disappointed that John was fading in popularity, as was their own influence. John the Baptist responded to his disciples this way:

> No one can receive anything except what has been given from heaven. You yourselves are my witnesses that I said 'I am not the Messiah, but I have been sent ahead of him.' He who has the bride is the bridegroom. The friend of the bridegroom, who stands and hears him, rejoices greatly at the bridegroom's voice. For this reason, my joy has been fulfilled. He must increase, but I must decrease. (John 3:28-30)

Not only did the influence of John the Baptist diminish, but he later was imprisoned and beheaded. (See Matthew 14:1-12.)

While you may not be called to be a martyr for your faith, you are called to the same process followed by John the Baptist. Christ must increase within you, and you must let go of your own image of yourself. This is difficult for all of us, but you should not fear taking this step. You will replace your flawed character with the flawless character of Christ. Make the exchange and allow the Lord to take over.

That's easy to say, but how do you actually do it? There are things you want to hold on to. You experience frequent temptations. Society pressures you to succeed and exalt yourself, caring little about your faith in the Lord. There is a way to defeat your ego, though: practice humility. This is a vital spiritual discipline.

In Matthew 23:12, Jesus teaches what we know in our hearts to be a great truth: "All who exalt themselves will be humbled, and all who humble themselves will be exalted." Numbers 12:3 tells us that one of the reasons God chose Moses to lead his people out of slavery in Egypt was his humility: "Now the man Moses was very humble, more so than anyone else on the face of the earth." If you are full of yourself, there is no room for God.

The key to suppressing your ego is to recognize that everything you have comes from Him. First Chronicles 29:14 states, "All things come from you Lord, and of your own have we given you." Perhaps you have had the good fortune to experience strong health, great physical ability, good looks, an accomplished career, financial success, or social popularity. When you are honest with yourself, though, you should recognize you had only a small—or no—part in these or other benefits or accomplishments. God provided the gifts and opportunities you needed to secure the blessings you now enjoy. Think about how quickly these could evaporate. In an instant, illness, injury, natural calamity, economic downturn or other unexpected events can change (or perhaps already have changed) the course of your life.

Almost every day we hear about car accidents, plane crashes, hurricanes, earthquakes, tornados or other accidents or natural disasters. I suspect your life, or the life of someone close to you, has been severely altered by a lost job, an injury, a heart attack, cancer, a natural disaster or some other misfortune.

As we addressed in Chapter Five, you are not in control—God is. This should greatly humble you, because if you approach these unexpected, life-changing events with honesty, it is difficult to explain how and why God allows them to occur. If you have had such an experience yourself, it is vital that you respond, not with bitterness and anger toward God, but with a humble spirit, open and receptive to what God will do through your change in circumstances. If you have not experienced such an event, I encourage you to spend time listening to someone who has and then turned to the Lord for strength and was restored. Proverbs 1:7 instructs, "The fear of the Lord is the beginning of knowledge: fools despise wisdom and instruction." Psalm 111:10 states, "The fear of the Lord is the beginning of wisdom; all those who practice it have a good understanding. His praise endures forever." And Psalm 112:1 states, "Praise the Lord! Happy are those who fear the Lord, who greatly delight in his commandments." We must be obedient to where God is directing us. Jesus is our example. Remember: from the cross came the resurrection, and out of tragedy and suffering can come renewal and new vitality.

The practice of humility also involves the suppression of your own pride when things are going your way. Whenever you attain a personal goal, or just have a good day, it's important to resist believing that you are responsible for that result. Suppress your pride, and give the credit to God. And examine the particular experience to see whether you recognize precisely how God was at work. How did He allow you to accomplish what you did? What gifts and talents has He given you? What events did He allow to take place? What other people were involved who were crucial to what occurred? This is how you genuinely grow in your relationship with the Lord and learn how to apply your faith. If you take all or most of the credit for your accomplishments (or blame others for your failures), you will miss the role that God played in the result and the growth in your relationship with Him will be hampered.

Please understand this does not mean that you simply do nothing and wait for the Lord to do it all instead. There is a balance you must achieve between the diligence in using the gifts He gave you and being humble in the use of those gifts. An excellent description of this balance is revealed to us in one of my favorite parables, often called "the Parable of the Talents," found in Mathew 25:14-30. Jesus teaches that God gives us all different gifts and calls us to make the most of those gifts for His glory. If you are not familiar with this story, I encourage you to study it, as it is a profound revelation of God's expectations:

> For it is as if a man, going on a journey, summoned his slaves and entrusted his property to them; to one he gave five talents, to another two, to another one, to each according to his ability. Then he went away. The one who had received the five talents went off at once and

traded with them, and made five more talents. In the same way, the one who had the two talents made two more talents. But the one who had received the one talent went off and dug a hole in the ground and hid his master's money. After a long time the master of those slaves came and settled accounts with them. Then the one who had received the five talents came forward, bringing five more talents, saying, 'Master, you handed over to me five talents; see, I have made five more talents.' His master said to him, 'Well done good and trustworthy slave; you have been trustworthy in a few things, I will put you in charge of many things; enter into the joy of your master.' And the one with the two talents also came forward, saying, 'Master, you have handed over to me two talents; see I have made two more talents.' His master said to him, 'Well done good and trustworthy slave; you have been trustworthy in a few things, I will put you in charge of many things, enter into the joy of your master.' Then the one who had received the one talent also came forward, saying 'Master, I knew that you were a harsh man, reaping where you did not sow, and gathering where you did not scatter seed; so I was afraid, and I went and hid your talent in the ground. Here you have what is yours.' But the master replied, 'You wicked and lazy slave! You knew, did you, that I reap where I did not sow, and gather where I did not scatter? Then you ought to have invested my money with bankers, and on my return I would have received what was my own with interest. So take the talent from him, and give it to the one with ten talents. For to all those who have, more will be given, and they will have an abundance; but from those who have nothing, even what they have will be taken away. As for this worthless slave, throw him into the outer darkness, where there will be weeping and gnashing of teeth.

I remember first hearing this parable and thinking that the master was awfully hard on the servant with one talent. He was given less than the others and certainly did not squander what he was given. It seems he may have acted a bit too cautiously. We would expect that wasting the gifts God has given us would anger Him, but here Jesus goes further by telling us that sitting on our gifts will greatly disappoint God. If we do not use them to support the kingdom of God, even what He has given us may be taken away.

The trustworthy servants, however, understood that their talents came from the master and that they were to be stewards of those talents. Acting with faith in the goodness and grace of their Provider, they were to make the most of the talents for the benefit of the master, to whom they understood they were accountable and to whom all the talents must be returned. They had no idea what their reward was to be, but the parable tells us the master then put them in charge of many more things, and they "entered into the joy of the master." They had a healthy respect for their master, which motivated them to do as much as they could with what they had been given.

By contrast, note that the servant with one talent is described as "wicked and lazy." He does not even try. He has no faith in his own ability and does not understand the true nature of his master, crippled by an "unhealthy fear" of and lack of respect for him. He takes no responsibility and actually blames the master for his lack of action by making accusations about the master's character, describing him as "harsh." The master responds that he at least should have put the talent in the bank and earned some interest. He then dismisses the servant into "the outer darkness, where there will be weeping and gnashing of teeth."

Look closely at the verse in this passage where Jesus states that "For to all those who have, more will be given, and they will have an abundance..." What a beautiful promise! The more faith we have and the more we apply it in using the gifts God has given us, the greater will be our strength and joy in Him. Jesus is revealing that God calls us not to be afraid, cautious and lazy, but rather to be obedient, diligent and productive for His glory.

With which servant do you most closely relate?

There is a balance between recognizing that all your gifts come from the Lord and a confidence in using those gifts to the best of your ability for His glory. The point in the context of this chapter is that your peace and strength come not from your abilities (which the parable clearly tells you come from

God and will vary from person to person), but from the faithful use of what God has given you. You must play the hand you have been dealt as best you can and not wish you had been dealt a better hand. Notice the servant with two talents did not sit around envying the servant with five. Also notice that more is expected of those who have been given more.

The understanding of these truths should lead you to be humble and joyful, not prideful and egotistical. When you accomplish your goals, you should recognize it is not what you have done, but rather what God has done through you with what He has given you. Your confidence comes from knowing that whatever challenges you may encounter, the Lord will take care of you, so long as you continue to be obedient to and trust in Him. In Romans 8:28, Paul states, "We know that all things work together for good for those who love God, who are called according to his purpose." The result is a joy that far exceeds any you could ever find from reliance on your own pride and ego, which is often based on the fragile and fleeting adulation of others.

Now, for you compulsive overachievers, the point of the Parable of the Talents is not to become a workaholic for God. Look at the implicit balance in the passage: five talents were turned into five more (not fifty or a hundred) and two talents were turned into two more (not twenty or forty). Pay close attention to what God is calling you to do, as opposed to what your ego is driving you to do.

Returning to the Galations 2:19-20 passage, there is one final message that directs you to the heart of the

Christian faith: the cross. You cannot address your own pride, ego, flaws or sins without understanding the power of the cross. It represents the central and most visible image of our faith. Jesus' crucifixion unleashed into the world a remarkable life-changing power. Paul teaches that the cross provides the power to rid yourself of selfish desires, personal ambitions and pride. The cross is where you find the will to be obedient and humble, and you learn that Christ is much more than just a great teacher and role model. He loved you and came to sacrifice himself for you. Even though He was the Son of God and completely innocent, with the power to save Himself, He humbled Himself completely and was perfectly obedient to the will of His Father in suffering brutal punishment and a painful death on the cross for all of us. How can anything you do ever approach what He did for you? Grasping the magnitude of that sacrifice should in itself humble you.

This Galatians passage reveals that Paul was not trying to imitate Christ and convince us how much he has accomplished in doing so, but rather he traded his entire life for a new one in which Christ was living in him with grace and power. While at first this may seem unachievable, it makes perfect sense if you think about it. You must let go of your own claim upon yourselves for the benefit of anyone except God. You need to sacrifice on the cross your own vision for where you want your life to go and turn it over to God. Oswald Chambers in his famous devotional book "My Utmost for his Highest" put it this way:

Am I willing to reduce myself to simply 'me'? Am I determined enough to strip myself of all that my friends think of me, and all that I think of myself? Am I willing and determined to hand over my simple naked self to God? Once I am, He will immediately sanctify me completely, and my life will be free from being determined and persistent toward anything except God.[3]

Are you ready to take this step and fully exchange your existing ego, pride and selfish desires for the joy, peace, freedom and abundance that Christ offers? If so, make the trade and move on to the last three steps on our journey. As we move toward the end, we will focus less on you and your relationship with the Lord, and more on how to use the power and strength of that relationship to love and encourage others in their own walk with the Lord. This will further strengthen you in your walk as He leads you along the path to your final destination: eternal life.

[3] Oswald Chambers, *My Utmost For His Highest*, An Updated Version in Today's Language, edited by James Reiman (Oswald Chambers Publications, Ltd., 1992).

Guiding Questions

1. What is your image of yourself? How much of this image is dependent on what other people think of you? How much of it is dependent on what God thinks of you?

2. Have you ever exalted yourself only to be humbled? In what areas of your life can you practice more humility?

3. What gifts and talents God has given you are you using for His glory? Are there gifts and talents God has given you which you have "buried" or are not fully utilizing?

Chapter Eight

Love

When the Pharisees heard that he had silenced the Sadducees, they gathered together, and one of them, a lawyer, asked him a question to test him. "Teacher, which commandment in the law is the greatest?" He said to him, "'you shall love the Lord your God with all your heart, and with all your soul, and with all your mind.' This is the greatest and first commandment. And a second is like it: 'You shall love your neighbor as yourself.' On these two commandments hang all the law and the prophets."

– Matthew 22:34-40 (See also Mark 12:28-31)

This is my commandment, that you love one another as I have loved you.

– John 15:12

I t is time to go in a different direction in your walk with the Lord. To this point, you have focused on understanding and strengthening your relationship with Him. The goal of the first seven steps was to establish a foundation of belief and faith in God and Jesus Christ and reliance upon the Holy Spirit. Accomplishing those goals includes reading and studying Scripture, prayer, obedience and practicing humility. I hope you are being transformed in this process, but if you have not already done so, you now should begin to shift focus from yourself and toward others in God's Kingdom. Your faith ultimately should cause you to look beyond yourself.

In the passages from Matthew and Mark referenced above, Jesus responds to the question of which commandment is the first and greatest by stating that there are two great commandments: love God and love your neighbor as yourself. At the heart of both is love. If you are to obey the two great commandments, you must understand love and have the capacity to both give and receive it. "We love because he first loved us" (1 John 4:19). Jesus directs us to simultaneously love God and our neighbor, and not one at the expense of the other. Developing a deep, abiding, prayerful, scripture-based relationship with the Lord has little meaning if it does not lead you to have compassion for and to actively care for others. Conversely, abundant good works alone will never fulfill you unless you are following the will of God. If you are instead following your own will or reacting to what others demand of you, your good works become misguided endeavors that sap your energy and eventually lead you away from God.

The love in the two great commandments is not detached and passive. This love is a verb, not a noun. None of the steps you have taken to this point will have much meaning, if they do not result in loving God and letting Him show you where and how to love others.

But what kind of love are we talking about? Does the Bible describe the love in the two great commandments and offer any real help in knowing how to participate in that love?

It does. Perhaps the most frequently read or heard biblical description of love is the one often read at weddings and found in 1 Corinthians 13 1-8:

If I speak in the tongues of mortals and of angels, but do not have love, I am but a noisy gong or a clanging cymbal. And if I have prophetic powers, and understand all mysteries and all knowledge, and if I have all faith, so as to remove mountains, but do not have love, I am nothing. If I give away all my possessions, and if I hand over my body so I may boast, but do not have love, I gain nothing.

Love is patient; love is kind; love is not envious or boastful or arrogant or rude. It does not insist on its own way; it is not irritable or resentful; it does not rejoice in wrongdoing, but rejoices in the truth. It bears all things, believes all things, hopes all things, endures all things. Love never ends.

In another well-known passage (Romans 8:37-39), Paul tells us:

No, in all these things we are more than conquerors through him who loved us. For I am convinced that neither death nor life, nor angels, nor rulers, nor things present, nor things to come, nor powers, nor height, nor depth, nor anything else in all creation, will be able to separate us from the love of God in Christ Jesus our Lord.

Society today has abundant focus on love, but not the kind called for in these passages. This creates confusion about the nature of love and how to give and receive it. We can learn from the Greek language here, as it uses at least three words to describe different kinds of love. *Eros* was the Greek word for romantic and sexual love or desire. The word "erotic" is derived from *eros*. Eros was the Greek god of love and the son of Aphrodite. *Philos* in Greek denotes fraternal love or the love of a friend. We know Philadelphia as the city of "brotherly love."

But the Greeks also had a third word for love: *agape*. It is a selfless and sacrificial love and is the kind Jesus, Paul and others are talking about in the passages set forth above. It is the unconditional love God has for us, which is best represented by the painful sacrifice of His only son, Jesus Christ, on the cross. This is a far different, deeper and greater love than romantic or fraternal love, which so often can be emotional, fleeting and conditional.

With only one word for love in the English language, the different natures are often misunderstood and confused. Humans have long misunderstood the nature of love and have tried to fulfill the need with romantic or fraternal love, when the only love that will permanently fill the void in their lives is the unconditional, never-ending, never-failing sacrificial love of God. Arguably, the root of many problems in our society can be traced to a severe shortage of *agape* love. This is a very rare commodity. Few are even exposed to it, much less taught how to give or receive it.

If you think about it, most of the love we give and receive does not approach the level of *agape*. In many marriages and families the love shown is largely conditional and infrequently sacrificial. This may explain why the divorce rate in the United States is so high. Husbands and wives will stay together as long as they receive what they need from the other. They ignore their wedding vows, which likely included a commitment to stay together "for better or worse, for richer or poorer and in sickness and in health as long as they both shall live." How many marriages could be saved by a period of unconditional, sacrificial love by one spouse for another during a difficult time or by a loving, Christ-centered support group holding a selfish, unloving spouse to a higher standard of love and obedience than currently demanded by our society? Many try to fill the void in their lives by pursuing the quick fix of a romantic relationship. In reality, though, romance provides only temporary solace and will never fill the emptiness in our lives—only God can do that through a relationship with Jesus Christ.

Much of the love between parents and children today also is conditional. Parents will love a child as long as the child is doing what the parent wants. It is easy to love children who are healthy and free from exceptional challenges, are making good grades, excelling in sports, and are popular with their peers. But in reality, raising children is hard work, requiring parents to commit the time it takes to love their children and help them work through the difficult times and decisions in their lives. Being a loving parent demands genuine sacrifice, whether it be in your job, social life, hobbies and interests, or whatever plans you may have for yourself. Parents should not delegate this great responsibility to someone else, and they should seek God's will—not their own—for their children.

On the other hand, one of the greatest examples of conditional love is that which children have for their parents, loving them when they get what they want, but withdrawing their love when the parents deny their requests. Ultimately, we hope our children will love and respect us, but much of that has to do with whether we are willing to endure the short term disapproval of our children in return for their ultimate respect for our decisions, which may not come for many years.

As a guide, we have the greatest example of a loving parent: God the Father. His love for us, His children, never ceases, no matter how far from Him we may stray. He is always waiting for us with open arms, and all we need to do is turn to Him and accept His love (read the familiar Parable of the Prodigal Son in Luke 15:11-32).

Many of us seek to fill the deep craving in our souls for love through our jobs, but much of the "love" or acceptance encountered in the workplace is conditional and fleeting. We feel "loved" when we do what our employer or colleagues want us to do, or even worse, when the bottom line justifies our continued employment. Many try to fulfill their need to be loved by seeking recognition and success in their jobs or careers, often at the sacrifice of their marriages and families. But remember what Jesus said in Mathew 16:26, which we addressed in Chapter Five: "What will it profit them if they gain the whole world, but lose their life?"

Still others rely primarily on social relationships as their source of love and fulfillment. While we may have some valuable friendships which are deep, abiding and sacrificial, many are superficial and fleeting and are dependent upon our engaging in a certain pattern of behavior. Many people substitute social recognition for genuine love. They spend significant time, energy and resources seeking the acceptance of others, without recognizing it will never fulfill them. I expect most of us have only a handful of true friends upon whom we can really rely in a crisis, and even those friendships will have their limitations. The love of God for us, however, has no limitations and never ceases. As Moses told the Israelites, "the Lord your God who goes with you; he will not fail you or forsake you" (Deuteronomy 31:6).

We also would like to think our churches would be a place where we find the *agape* love of God readily available. In the healthiest of churches, you will find people truly ministering to each other in a loving and transforming way; but regrettably this is often not the case. Many attending church today are hungry for a deeper relationship with God, but are not receiving the attention they need. Many churches simply are not in the business of leading their congregations to actively minister to each other and their communities in an open, vibrant, loving and sacrificial way based on the Gospel of Jesus Christ. In some churches, divorce, adultery, addiction, abuse and other forms of brokenness are found among the members without the church providing the means to address them.

Worshipping God in church with fellow Christians is, of course, a vital part of your spiritual growth, and I strongly encourage regular worship; but your journey will depend upon your connection to a church and other ministries that have as their principal focus your knowledge of and commitment to Jesus Christ. When selecting a church, in addition to strong preaching and fellowship, look for active adult Sunday School programs, Bible studies, small groups, mission work, and the planting of new churches. I believe the most important test of a healthy church or ministry Is whether you see lives being truly changed by the love of Christ acting through those involved.

So how do you practice the kind of love called for by Jesus? You need to discover the kind of sacrificial, transforming and powerful love Jesus first showed you by sacrificing Himself on the cross. In John 15:13 (the verse following the one quoted at the beginning this chapter) Jesus tells His disciples: "No one has greater love than this, to lay down one's life for one's friends." This kind of love will not only transform those who receive it from you, but also will transform you as you learn to give it. In Luke 6:27 — part of the Sermon on the Mount — Jesus describes in detail the kind of love he requires:

> But I say to you that listen, love your enemies, do good to those who hate you, bless those who curse you, pray for those who abuse you. If anyone strikes you on the cheek, offer the other also; and from anyone who takes away your coat do not withhold even your shirt. Give to anyone who begs from you; and if anyone takes away your goods, do not ask for them again. Do to others as you would have them do to you.

Yes, if you did not know it before, Jesus Christ is the source of the so-called "Golden Rule." Notice the absence of conditions for the giving of the love described in this passage. There is no requirement that your enemies first apologize or that one who is in great need meet certain criteria before you reach out and help them. While what Jesus calls you to do in this passage may seem quite challenging, what He is saying is Christian love is not just a feeling—it requires action. Our relationship with the Lord has little meaning if it does not first change us so we can change the lives of others.

One way to change others is to love them sacrificially and unconditionally, thereby demonstrating the kind of love that Jesus had for all of us. This does not mean you love others without a measure of discipline and accountability. Loving an alcoholic does not mean giving him or her another drink. Loving your children does not always mean you give them whatever it takes to make them happy. Proverbs 13:24 says, "Those who spare the rod hate their children, but those who love them are diligent to discipline them." Loving others does not mean being completely accepting and tolerant of everything they may do. That would likely not put you in a position to transform someone's life. You cannot always avoid difficult issues or circumstances involving those you love, but rather, with the Lord providing guidance and strength you may be called to confront those difficult circumstances. You may have to expend significant time, patience, understanding and prayer to ascertain a solution. You then may be required to lovingly confront someone with a difficult message they do not want to hear. In those circumstances, be prepared to have the patience to properly minister to the person, and always work to follow God's will rather than your own.

The capacity for sacrificial love initially may be affected by how much you have received in your own life. For some it comes easily, as if they were born with an unlimited reservoir of *agape* love. Others may have been denied the love of their parents, a spouse, siblings or friends, or were even abused as a child or a spouse. For them to find the capacity to openly love others may be more difficult. You have the capacity to be transformed, however, if you accept that God loves you completely and that nothing you can do will ever cause Him to withdraw that love. When you sin, all you have to do is repent and turn to Him.

Jesus says the first critical step in learning how to love others is to love God "with all of your heart, with all your soul, and with all your mind and with all your strength" (Mark 12:30). You must turn every part of your life over to Him: your emotions (heart), your spiritual life (soul), your intellect (mind) and your strength (physical body). No matter what your circumstances, God is in the midst of them lovingly working out His will for good. You must resist the temptation to question that He is not there. Once you put your complete faith in God, you are free to receive His unconditional love, and to allow that love to flow through you to others. If His love stops with you, that love becomes like a stagnant pond. If, however, His love flows through you, it becomes like a clear, refreshing, mountain stream cleansing all it touches as it cascades down. In John 4:13, Jesus said to the Samaritan woman He met at the well, "Everyone who drinks this water will be thirsty again, but those who drink of the water that I will give them will never be thirsty. The water that I will give will become in them a spring of water gushing up to eternal life." In John 7:38 Jesus said, "Let anyone who is thirsty come to me, and let the one who believes in me drink. As scripture has said, 'Out of the believer's heart shall flow rivers of living water.'" A crucial element of that "living water" is the *agape* love of God. As you share that "water" with others, God's love and light will flow through you to them, simultaneously nourishing, cleansing and purifying both you and them.

Turn your relationship with the Lord into action by loving others as God has loved you. You will find joy, peace, fulfillment and inspiration. You will also be laying the foundation for our next step: sharing your faith with others. Those to whom you are ministering, who do not know the Lord, may first need to know you and the Lord love them unconditionally before you will be able to lead them to their own encounter with Jesus Christ. Once you experience the unconditional, enduring love of God given through Jesus, you will want to share this joyful gift with others.

It is critical to understand why and how to bring others into a relationship with the Lord. When you love and want to help someone who is in need, there is so much *you* want to *do*, but you are not in control and have your limitations. The love and power of God have no limitations. You will see there is no greater gift you can give than the knowledge and love of God, his Son, and the fellowship of the Holy

Spirit. Take the next step in our journey so you will know how to play your part in delivering this great gift to others, which may do far more for them than you could ever imagine.

Guiding Questions

1. What are the sources of love in your life? Into which category of love do they fall—*eros, philios* or *agape*?

2. What do you consider to be the greatest act of unconditional love you have ever seen or experienced? What was its effect on you?

3. What circumstances in your life could improve by your practice of unconditional love? Are you able to give that kind of love? If not, why not? Is there a way God could help you give it?

Chapter Nine

Make Disciples

Go therefore and make disciples of all
nations, baptizing them in the name of the
Father and of the Son and of the Holy Spirit,
and teaching them to obey everything that I
have commanded you. And remember, I am
with you always, to the end of the age.

– Mathew 28:19-20

As his departing message in the last two verses
of his Gospel, Matthew conveys this command
of Jesus to his disciples: go and make new disciples,
teaching them all Jesus had taught. Fortunately for
us, those disciples followed that command. Look at
the results: from the humble beginnings of a small
band of unassuming and impoverished followers, the
good news of Jesus Christ has been spread over the
entire world. You and I are the beneficiaries of the

committed, courageous and sacrificial acts of the first disciples.

All of them, except John, were martyred for their faith, along with John the Baptist and the Apostle Paul. These devoted and brave followers, as well as the many others who sacrificed their lives for their belief in Jesus, would not have died for something that was not true. As the result of their commitment and sacrifice, we in the United States, and many others across the globe, are free to spread the news about Jesus without risking our lives. What if Matthew, Mark, Luke, John, Peter, Paul and the many other devoted followers had been unwilling to risk sharing what they believed about Jesus Christ?

Look back on the steps you have taken so far: if you believe in God, that Jesus Christ is his Son, that the Bible reveals God's truth and that the Father and Son and the Holy Spirit are transforming your life, how can you possibly keep that good news to yourself? One meaning of the word Gospel is "good news," and it is natural to want to share good news with others. When you have any other good news such as a marriage, the birth of a child, a new job or a promotion, a new home, a new car, etc., you want to tell others all about it. But what better news can you impart to others than that Jesus Christ died on the cross for them and their sins are forgiven? They are relieved from striving to be good enough; all they have to do is believe in Him.

Knowing Jesus and allowing Him and the Holy Spirit into your life helps everything else make sense. This is not just one solution among many others; it is *the* solution—the very key to life itself. In Colossians 1:26 and 27, Paul describes it as "the mystery that has been hidden throughout the ages and generations but has now been revealed to his saints." This great mystery has been revealed to you. How can you keep such a wonderful gift to yourself? If Jesus died a tor- turous death on the cross for you and for me, and His disciples were martyred for their commitment to Him, the very least we can do is tell others about it.

If you care about those you love and who are in need, you should want to give them the remarkable gift of an encounter with Jesus Christ. You often want to fix other people's problems—and there certainly may be some things you could and should do to help others in need—but the Lord can do vastly more than you ever imagined. He can love, heal, console, guide, grant wisdom and perform miracles in ways far beyond your capabilities. And if you pay careful attention to how He is working in your life and in the lives of others, He will grant you the privilege of becoming the instrument through which He works.

Jesus expressly calls you to action in sharing your faith with others. In Matthew 5:13-16, Jesus said,

> You are the salt of the earth, but if salt has lost its taste, how can its saltiness be restored? It is no longer good for anything, but is thrown out and trampled underfoot.

> You are the light of the world. A city built on a hill cannot be hid. No one after lighting a lamp puts it under the bushel basket, but

on the lamp stand, and it gives light to all in the house. In the same way, let your light shine before others, so that they may see your good works and give glory to your Father in heaven.

Throughout the Gospels, Jesus makes repeated references to light. It is a powerful metaphor for what belief in God and Jesus Christ can do in our lives and in the lives of others. Think of what light does to darkness—it instantly dispels it. Have you stumbled around in a dark house after the electricity has gone off and finally found a candle? Do you recall the feeling of relief when the candle is lit, and there is a glimmer of light in what previously was total darkness? While wind or other external forces may extinguish the candle, the darkness itself cannot overcome it. Think of yourself as that candle and how you can be a light in the spiritual darkness of others. Jesus is the initial light in our darkness, but he calls us to light as many other candles as we can before ours is finally extinguished. In 2 Corinthians 4-6, Paul states,

And even if our gospel is veiled, it is veiled to those who are perishing. In their case, the god of the world has blinded the minds of unbelievers, to keep them from seeing the light of the gospel of the glory of Christ, who is the image of God. For we do not proclaim ourselves; we proclaim Jesus Christ as Lord and ourselves as slaves for Jesus' sake. For it is the God who said, "Let light shine out ot darkness," who has shone in our hearts to give the light of knowledge of the glory of God in the face of Jesus Christ.

What keeps us from being a light to others? For many of us, it is difficult. We are unable to do it or believe we cannot share our experience effectively. There are many obstacles to the sharing of our faith. Some are created by our culture and some are part of our natural human condition. We need to be aware of them so we can overcome them. Fortunately, Jesus knew we would face these challenges and directly addressed them in His teachings. I encourage you to read carefully each of the obstacles briefly discussed below and see whether any applies to you. All of them have hindered me at times in my journey.

Excuses. One of the first things we often do is make excuses for why we cannot spend time with the Lord or spread his Word. We frequently believe we have something else we should be doing. We lead busy lives and have many responsibilities—jobs, families, homes and civic and social obligations. The Parable of the Great Dinner (Luke 14:15-24) examines what Jesus says about those who do not respond to his call because they believe they have other more important things to do first. In Luke 9:57-62, He confronts some of the excuses given, including burying one's father or saying farewell to one's family. Jesus says, "No one who puts a hand to the plow and looks back is fit for the kingdom of God." We need to understand that when Jesus calls us to action he means *now* is the time, regardless of what else we think we have to do. When God reveals that you have an opportunity to be a light to others who are in spiritual darkness, put aside your excuses and seize the moment, or the moment may be lost.

Fear. As we discussed in Chapter Five, many of us fear turning to God. We want to be in control. We are afraid of what might happen if we release everything to Him. We think a better plan is to control as much as we can and turn to Him when things get really bad. The problem with that is that when the crisis comes we have not sufficiently practiced our faith in the Lord and are unable to rely upon it. We panic and turn to our own natural resources, which frequently are inadequate. Read the account of Jesus calming the storm while in the boat with His disciples, which appears in Matthew 8:23-27, Mark 4:35-41 and Luke 8:22-25. In Mark 4:40, Jesus challenged the disciples: "Why are you afraid? Have you still no faith?"

Fear of trusting and turning our entire lives over to God is often the root cause of not sharing our faith with others. If we think we can solve some of our problems without God, why would we challenge others to put their complete faith in Him?

We also fear the consequences of telling others we are a Christian and offering Jesus Christ as the solution to their difficulties. We are concerned that they will think us odd and that it will chill or end our relationship with them. We fear they will reject both us and the message.

But God loves you unconditionally (and will take care of you). This should inspire you to overcome any fears of what others may think. Our God is good and your efforts to help others by directing them to Him will be rewarded, although the rewards and the results may not be immediate.

If you are following God's will, the opinions of others should not matter. As your faith grows, you increasingly live in God's will and strength and not your own. In my case, God increasingly strengthened me in the midst of difficult circumstances, yet all around me people I cared for were broken and troubled. I finally reached a place where I wanted to share my faith with them, so they could know the same peace, comfort, love and joy I had found. I knew Jesus Christ could transform their lives in remarkable ways, if only they would turn to Him. As I stated in the introduction, this is one reason I felt called to write this book.

We all have different gifts, talents and experiences. God may call you to share your faith in your particular way. It could be through teaching, speaking, music, missionary work, service to the poor or a multitude of other callings. You know the gifts God has given you. What matters is you use, not squander, those gifts to His glory. And when you use those gifts to share your faith with others, you will be given opportunities and experiences beyond what you could ever imagine.

Concern over results. Often we obsess over what the results of sharing our faith will be. We live in an achievement- and success-oriented society, but God's ways are much different from those of our culture. We need to alter our worldly perspective and cease fretting about immediate results in particular situations or the mere number of people we are trying to bring to know the Lord.

I encourage you to study Jesus' teaching in the Parable of the Sower (Mark 4:1-20 or Luke 8:4-18). You will learn it is up to us to sow the seeds, but the harvest is up to God. Not all the seeds fall on fertile ground or grow as quickly as we would like. You simply plant, water, weed and fertilize, then leave the results to God.

You often may wish to control the process and the timetable, but you need to allow God to work, and provide the support when He calls you to do so. One of the best ways is to pray unceasingly for those to whom you are ministering.

You can also encourage someone seeking answers to questions about faith in a variety of ways. Take them to church, and they may just hear a sermon that carries them to the next step in their own journey. You can suggest reading a Christian book and even give them a copy. Reading *Mere Christianity* and *Abide in Christ,* both recommended to me by others, were vital in developing and strengthening my relationship with Jesus Christ. You can direct people to musical performances, dinners, luncheons, service projects, mission trips, Bible studies, and small groups, all of which may provide enlightenment, encouragement and strength in the way of the Lord. What you do and the way you live your life may inspire someone to follow the path of the Lord without your even being aware of it. My life was transformed by a friend taking me to a luncheon where I met others who would ultimately lead me to turn my entire life over to Jesus. Always be prepared to encourage someone else in their own journey.

Recognize, however, the challenge of balancing boldness in sharing your faith with humility before God. Sharing your faith is not about you and your gifts; it is about the person to whom you are ministering. You must meet them where are, not where you are. Pay attention, listen, be sensitive and compassionate toward their needs, waiting for an opportunity to lovingly tell them what you believe. This is a refined skill which takes practice and experience. Do not be discouraged if you do not say or do the right thing at exactly the right time. God is at work. The seed has been planted. There likely will be other opportunities for you or others to nurture the growth of that seed. We should take solace in remembering that it is our job to plant the seeds, while the harvest is up to God.

As with other undertakings in life, there also will be times when you will be flatly rejected. Do not be discouraged. As Christ told his disciples in Mathew 10:14-15, "shake the dust off your feet" and just move on. The Lord may be telling you there is more fertile ground elsewhere to sow the seeds of faith.

Put aside your fears and excuses—make yourself available. Listen to God and allow Him to use you and your gifts for His glory. There is no greater joy than knowing God has used you to bring someone else to know Jesus Christ.

Let us now move on to our final destination. While we will be taking our last step on our journey with the Lord, it also will lead us back to our starting point, as it provides the inspiration for and the backdrop against which we take every other step. We now push ahead to the end where we look beyond this world toward the promise of eternal life.

Guiding Questions

1. What keeps you from sharing your faith in the Lord with others? Make a list of any obstacles and consider how you might overcome them.

2. What can you do to prepare yourself to share your faith with others? What gifts has God given you that could be used as a means of glorifying Him in sharing your faith?

3. Think of people who would benefit from coming to know the Lord. Consider how you may be able to effectively share your belief in the Lord with them. And when you're ready, do it!

Chapter Ten

Eternal Life

Do not store up for yourselves treasures on earth where moth and rust consume and where thieves break in and steal; but store up for yourselves treasures in heaven, where neither moth nor rust consume and where thieves do not break in and steal. For where your treasure is, there will your heart be also.
– Matthew 6:19-21

God has built one great certainty into His design and into your journey with Him. Sooner or later, one way or another, you are going to die. No matter how hard you work at preventing it, one day your physical body is going to cease operating. It might be tomorrow or it might be decades from now, but it will happen, regardless of the amount of control you think you have over "your world." You may think you are a pretty big deal, but in the big picture of things you are just like everyone else. "You are dust and to dust you shall return" (Genesis 3:19).

As we have already discussed, God is in control of your life and your eternal existence. He is The Big Deal. He is The Creator. He controls The Big Picture, while at the same time is involved in tiniest details of your life. He created you, and He cares deeply about you.

In Psalm 139:7-12, David, the great King of Israel, wrote:

Where can I go from your spirit?
  Or where can I flee from your presence?
If I ascend to heaven you are there;
  if I make my bed is Sheol, you are there.
If I take the wings of the morning
  and settle at the farthest limits of the sea,
even there your hand shall lead me,
  and your right hand shall hold me fast.

In Matthew 10:29-31 Jesus said, "Are not two sparrows sold for a penny? Yet not one of them will fall to the ground apart from your Father. And even the hairs of your head are all counted. So do not be afraid; you are of more value than many sparrows."

Based on these and many other passages, you know at this point in your journey that a) God created you, b) God is control of your life, and c) God loves you and everything about you. With this knowledge, have you faced the reality that when you die God will decide where you spend eternity? If not, now is the time. Your journey with the Lord will not be concluded until you wrestle with this reality. If you take the time to consider it, I assume you will choose an eternal life with God over the alternative.

We do not like to talk about death or its consequences, but it was a central focus of Jesus' life and teachings. Look closely at John 3:16, which is perhaps the most widely publicized verse in the New Testament. John reveals that one of the principal reasons Jesus came to this world is to give us the opportunity for eternal life: "For God so loved the world that he gave his only Son, so that everyone who *believes* in him may not perish but may have *eternal life*" (emphasis mine). God gives us a simple formula for eternal life: Believe in His Son Jesus Christ, and you will have eternal life.

The alternative appears to be that you will perish.

Jesus taught frequently about death and eternal life. Look at the following passages:

> Very truly, I tell you, unless a grain of wheat falls into the earth and dies, it remains just a single grain; but if it dies, it bears much fruit. Those who love their life lose it, and those who hate their life in this world will keep it for eternal life. Whoever serves me must follow me, and where I am, there will my servant be also. Whoever serves me the Father will honor. (John 12:24-26)

> Then Jesus said to his disciples, "Truly I tell you it will be hard for a rich person to enter the kingdom of heaven. Again I tell you, it is

easier for a camel to go through the eye of a needle than for someone who is rich to enter the kingdom of God." When the disciples heard this they were greatly astounded and said, "Then who can be saved?" But Jesus looked at them and said, "For mortals it is impossible, but for God all things are possible." (Mathew 19:23-26)

Blessed are you when people hate you, and when they exclude you, and defame you on account of the Son of Man. Rejoice in that day and leap for joy, for surely your reward is great in heaven; for that is what your ancestors did to the prophets. (Luke 6:22-23)

These are only some of the many passages in which Jesus teaches about eternal life and the kingdom of heaven. The Gospels are replete with teachings and parables about the subject. (Read also John 17:1-3, John 3:11-15, and Mark 10:17-22.)

These passages explain that when we die, we will be judged by the Lord. There are consequences to our behavior and actions on earth. Paul said in 2 Corinthians 5:10, "For all of us must appear before the judgment seat of Christ, so that each of us may receive recompense for what has been done in the body, whether good or evil."

Not everyone makes the cut, and there is a distinct alternative to spending eternity with God in the heavenly kingdom for those who are excluded. Jesus makes it very clear we will be held accountable for what we have done and what we have not done, and God requires more than just sitting around and not doing anything wrong. We must believe in Jesus and act on that belief. Remember what Jesus said in the Parable of the Talents about the slave who buried his one talent (which we examined in Chapter Seven): "As for this worthless slave, throw him into the outer darkness, where there will be weeping and gnashing of teeth" (Matthew 25:29-30). Read carefully the passage immediately following that one in which Jesus describes how and on what basis we will be judged by Him (Matthew 25:31-46). He will "separate people one from another as the shepherd separates the sheep from the goats, and he will put the sheep at his right hand and the goats at the left" (verses 32-33). Those on his right hand, the righteous, will "be blessed by my Father and inherit the kingdom prepared for you from the foundation of the world" (verse 35). But those on his left hand, the accursed, "will go away into eternal punishment" (verse 46).

While these passages may invoke fear about our eternal destination, our focus should be on the joy of the rewards we will receive in the next life. Before we get there, we will face challenges, crisis, pain and tribulation in some form. We cannot fully explain how or why difficult or tragic circumstances occur. It is our response to them that determines how we will be judged by the Lord.

The best way to live a truly holy and sacrificial life on earth is to recognize that our reward is not here, but in the life to come. And it will be greater than anything we can imagine. Living our worldly lives in the context of our heavenly lives and rewards provides the perspective and the strength to endure, sacrifice and serve in ways far beyond what we could hope to do if we rely solely on being rewarded in this world.

I ask you to stop and think about how much more you could endure and how much you could and would do for others if you focused on heavenly rewards rather than on how your choices will affect you in this world. How much more of your financial resources would you give to others in need if you were more concerned with your heavenly retirement than with your earthly retirement? Would a heavenly perspective alter how much time you spend working, watching television or pursuing personal success, social acceptance or your hobbies?

How do you think Jesus endured the remarkable unfairness and brutality inflicted upon Him here on earth? He was a wholly innocent victim, tortured and put to an excruciating death on the cross as a punishment for healing the sick and teaching the truth about God. The only way He could have endured such injustice and inequity was to know He was doing what God called Him to do in this world. Jesus knew His reward would be great in heaven. The same must have been true for the disciples who were martyred for their belief in Jesus. In Mark 10:43-45, Jesus stated, "...whoever wishes to become great among you must be your servant, and whoever wishes to be first among you must be the slave of all. For the Son of Man came not to be served but to serve, and to give his life a ransom for many."

The concept of changing your behavior now in exchange for rewards later in heaven is challenging to both grasp and implement. I continue to struggle with this perspective. One book that has been very helpful to me is *A Life God Rewards* by Bruce Wilkinson. He states, "You see, Jesus isn't asking you and me to enjoy misery on His behalf. Instead He's saying that the consequences in heaven for certain actions on earth will be so wonderful that simply knowing they're coming—and knowing that they will be great—can transform how we live now. Yes, even create spontaneous outbursts of joy."[4]

A large part of what we are trying to accomplish by taking the ten steps in this book is to transform your life through your belief in God and his Son Jesus Christ. Wilkinson believes your faith and focus on eternity and its rewards can radically change your behavior and your life. He states, "Simple decisions, such as how you spend your time and money will become opportunities of great promise. And you will begin to live with an unshakeable certainty that everything you do today matters forever."[5] I encourage you to read Wilkinson's book and continue to study and explore how belief in eternity and its rewards can transform your life in the here and now.

Finally, our greatest hope and inspiration to live a life of faith in an eternal relationship with Jesus is found in the Resurrection. His entire life—from con-

---

[4] Bruce W. Wilkinson, with David Kopp, *A Life God Rewards* (Multnomah Publishers, Inc. 2002 by Expotential, Inc.), page 11.

[5] Ibid, page 16.

ception and virgin birth, to the healing of the sick, to His other miracles (including the raising of Lazarus from the dead), to His voluntary sacrificial death for us on the cross—leads to the Resurrection. It is what sets the Christian faith apart from all others. We must believe and put our hope in the Resurrection in order for the rest of our faith to have meaning. Each day we must embrace the unsurpassable joy of Easter. The New Testament is not a story and commentary upon a great teacher or prophet and his ethical and moral teachings; it is the account of the Son of God coming to earth, revealing the truth about His Father, dying an unjust death as a sacrifice for us, and then overcoming that death by rising from the dead to be with God and reign forever.

Jesus' Resurrection provides us hope and joy on at least two levels. First, we may live on earth knowing that belief in Him grants us eternal life with the Father. That eternal, heavenly existence will not only be much better than our life in this broken world, it will be a life of peaceful, loving perfection. There will be no anxiety, stress, jealously, envy or greed. I like to think of the most joyous moments I have had on earth (such as the birth of a child, a perfect golf shot, a beautiful spring day, surfing the perfect wave, a spectacular sunset, or the excitement of a child on Christmas morning) and believe that in heaven we will be permanently in that state of joy, without any inhibiting or destructive earthly forces leading us astray.

Secondly, the Resurrection reveals to us the means by which we may know the kingdom of heaven here on earth. When we set aside our will and submit to God's, we are transformed to a new life. It can follow the same natural process of the seed that is planted in the earth and dies, only to live again to grow into a thriving plant bearing abundant fruit or a colorful flower. A caterpillar must develop a cocoon before it can transform into a butterfly. Grapes must be crushed and squeezed before they can become fine wine. Think of the miracle of these natural processes and understand God is calling us to do the same thing. We must go through our own crucifixion before we can be resurrected.

You may have to endure pain and suffering so that you can be reborn into a new life (think how an emerging butterfly breaks out of its cocoon), but just as it was for Jesus, the transformation into a resurrected, eternal life will be worth the pain. You may have to undergo many crucifixions over the course of your life, but none will approach the pain and suffering He endured to make available to you the joy of resurrection into eternal life with Him and the Father. I urge you to watch and carefully reflect upon the movie *The Passion of Christ* to get a sense of the unjustified punishment and torture to which Jesus voluntarily submitted for you.

Through His Resurrection, Jesus conquered death, so you no longer have to fear it. You are instead free to focus on eternal life, knowing it is there if you only believe in Him who opened the door. But make no mistake about the importance of this step. You must believe in the Resurrection. It is the defining event of the Christian faith. You cannot take any of the other steps we have discussed or follow any other paths in your journey without taking this step. All of it leads you to this final destination and if you do not accept the Resurrection, you will be walking in a confusing maze without the true hope of finding your way and completing your journey. You cannot accept the celebration of Christmas without also accepting Good Friday and embracing Easter. In 1 Corinthians 15:13-14 Paul states, "If there is no resurrection of the dead, then Christ has not been raised, and if Christ has not been raised, then our proclamation has been in vain and your faith has been in vain."

The end of your journey and your final resting place is everlasting life. Your life in this world committed to Jesus Christ should be preparation for the next life. As Paul stated in Philippians 3:10-11: "I want to know Christ, and the power of his resurrection and the sharing of his sufferings by becoming like him in his death, if somehow I may attain the resurrection of the dead." Jesus died for you on the Cross and was resurrected, thereby conquering death so you do not have to fear it. All you have to do is believe, which brings you back to where you began your journey.

I pray the steps you have taken along the path of your journey with the Lord will transform your life and lead you to a day by day, moment by moment, walk with Jesus Christ guided by the Holy Spirit.

"The grace of the Lord Jesus Christ, the love of God, and the communion of the Holy Spirit be with all of you." (2 Corinthians 13:13)

Guiding Questions

1. What is your view of heaven? What is your view of the alternative? How do you believe the Lord determines who spends eternity with Him?

2. Does a true belief in everlasting life change your actions and behavior on earth? For example, does it change how you approach financial matters or your relationships with others?

3. What personal crucifixions and resurrections have you had in your life? Can you see the hand of God at work in them?

CPSIA information can be obtained at www.ICGtesting.com
Printed in the USA
LVOW07s0226181114

414245LV00001B/23/P